Where to Start – Divorce

How to Successfully Navigate Your Way Through Divorce

Elena M. Greenberg

Copyright (c) 2023 Elena M. Greenberg, Where to Start Books LLC
All rights reserved.

No part of this publication or the information in it may be quoted from or reproduced in any form by means such as printing, scanning, photocopying or otherwise without prior written permission of the copyright holder.

ISBN 979-8-9881023-0-4

Get Your Free Gift!

As a thank you for reading my book, I'd like to gift you a downloadable PDF workbook to help you navigate your specific situation. You can get your copy here:

https://www.wheretostartbooks.com/divorce-workbook/

Table of Contents

Introduction vii
How to Use this Book ix

Chapter 1: Choosing an Attorney 1
Chapter 2: Divorce Models 11
Chapter 3: Fee Structures 15
Chapter 4: Representing Yourself 21
Chapter 5: Children and Divorce 23
Chapter 6: The Divorce Process - An Overview 27
Chapter 7: The Divorce Process - Beginning Stage 33
Chapter 8: The Divorce Process - Middle Stage 37
Chapter 9: The Divorce Process - End Stage 43
Chapter 10: The Divorce Process - After the Divorce 49
Chapter 11: Basics of Court Etiquette 57
Chapter 12: Other Professionals 63
Chapter 13: Safety and Wellness 71
Chapter 14: Frequently Asked Questions 81

What's Next? 89
Glossary of Terms 91
About The Author 113

Introduction

"Knowledge is power."
Francis Bacon

Jane is getting a divorce, but she doesn't know how or where to start. She doesn't want anyone to know about the divorce until she has a plan in place, especially not her kids. Jane knows she will need an attorney, but she does not want to ask friends or family for a recommendation, so she starts by looking up attorneys online. She has no idea how to choose an attorney, so she just goes with the first one she finds that practices family law, looks like they have some experience, and offers a free consultation.

Jane is nervous about meeting with an attorney. She has so many questions about the divorce process that she doesn't think about what she wants to know about the attorney. Jane meets with an older male attorney. He has more than twenty years of experience in family law, and he looks like he would be very intimidating in a courtroom. Even though she is hoping that she and her spouse will not have to go to trial, she thinks these attributes make this attorney a good choice. Jane is intimidated by this attorney and finds it hard to talk to him about her personal situation, but she believes this would be a silly reason not to hire him.

The attorney gives her an overview of what the divorce process will look like. He does not ask her about her goals, nor does he offer her any choices. Jane is left with the impression that there are no choices she can make in the divorce process and that what the attorney describes is how her divorce will have to go. He quotes her a large retainer and gives her some paperwork to fill out if she wants to hire him.

Jane leaves feeling overwhelmed. Much of what the attorney told her she either did not understand or can't remember. Jane decides to hire him because she does not want to go through another consultation. She thinks that all attorneys will be the same and that her choice of attorney won't make any difference on how her divorce will go.

Jane feels powerless over her own divorce.

If Jane had picked up this book first, she would know that she has many choices. She could read about the different divorce models in chapter 2 and choose the one that best fits her goals and her family. She could review the different fee structures in chapter 3 and find one that would best fit her budget. In chapter 1, she would learn alternative ways to find an attorney without having to ask friends and family or picking at random from the Internet. Chapter 1 would also give her information on how to choose an attorney and what questions to ask before hiring. She would have an overview of the divorce process, an easy-to-consult glossary of terms, and information about other professionals who might be useful to her during this process. The knowledge in this book would have empowered Jane to make her own choices rather than feeling powerless in the divorce process.

***

In over 14 years of practice, I have represented hundreds of people through the divorce process. I have witnessed again and again what it is like for my clients to be overwhelmed as they try to navigate a confusing and opaque legal system.

I wrote this book to be a roadmap to guide you through the divorce process. You will still need a car and, likely, a driver to get through it, but at least you will know where you are going and be able to choose the route. With the help of this book, you will even recognize some of the landmarks along the way.

How to Use this Book

This book is like having a lawyer at your fingertips without the hourly charge! You can refer to this book as a place to start when you are looking for:

- help with finding, choosing, and preparing for your first meeting with an attorney.
- information about different divorce models so you can choose the right divorce model for your situation and for your family.
- a better understanding of fee structures and what options you have in financing your divorce.
- definitions of legal terms that you are not familiar with or want to refresh your understanding.
- guidance in preparing for your first court hearing.

When clients first come to me, they usually have no idea what the divorce process is going to be like. They don't know what kind of divorce they want, or even that there are options for them to consider. They don't know how to choose an attorney, or what to do next. Not only will this book give you a better idea of what you want and how to achieve it, but your general knowledge of the process will empower you to find the attorney and model of divorce that is the right fit for you.

The beginning stages of contemplating or starting a divorce are overwhelming. The stress of your situation can be a barrier to processing and retaining the information you gather. In addition to overload and stress, the legal aspects of divorce are hard to understand. Lawyers go to law school for three years to understand the legal system, and they are required to take a specific amount of continued education every year. Despite all that education and years of experience, family law can be difficult even for attorneys, especially if that is not a primary area of practice for them. The advantage of having this book is that you won't have to try to absorb it in one sitting. You can revisit the sections of this book that are relevant to your case, over and over again, without racking up a hefty legal bill.

Unless you have a flat fee arrangement, your attorney will charge you for every text, email, or phone call you make. Even if you do have a flat fee arrangement, there may be limits to how much attorney time you have access to. Most attorneys charge by the tenth of the hour. For example, if your attorney charges $300 an hour, every time you send an email to ask what a term means or what to expect next, they will likely charge you $30 for that email, more than the cost of this book. Some attorneys have a minimum charge of two tenths of an hour, which means that same email can cost you $60 or more.

On the other hand, not asking your attorney about things that you need to know can make things worse. You should have open communication with your attorney so that you know what your specific rights and options are during your divorce. You do not want to find yourself going through your divorce blindly with the increased anxiety of the unknown. This book will allow you to save money while being fully informed of the process and your options, thereby reducing your anxiety and improving the outcome of your divorce.

The chapters are organized in the order of the information people tend to want to know first, not by the importance of the topics. The relative level of importance of each topic will be unique to your situation.

The first chapter deals with finding and choosing an attorney who is right for you. You may want to meet with an attorney first and get their guidance on what divorce model to pursue and what fee structure would work best for you, and then read the chapters about divorce models and fees. Or, you may want to know what the overall process looks like before you think about what to look for in an attorney or choosing a divorce model.

There is no need to read this book from cover to cover. If you want a collaborative divorce, but you are not sure exactly what a collaborative divorce entails, read chapter 2 first. If you know what kind of divorce you want but not how to choose a suitable attorney, start in chapter 1. Maybe you are in the middle of divorce proceedings and have been told you need to attend mediation, but you don't know what mediation is; turn to chapter 8 and page 102. Likely the documents you receive include terms or abbreviations you are not familiar with; check the glossary of terms at the end of the book. You might have a pretrial conference coming up and your attorney is telling you not to worry about it and that preparation is unnecessary. However, you are going to be stressed out until you know more about it or about proper etiquette during the hearing; you can find out what a pretrial conference is in the glossary of terms and read about etiquette in chapter 11.

You will still need to ask your attorney clarifying questions about how things will work in your specific case and in your specific jurisdiction. However, having the foundation information in this book will make it easier for your attorney to explain and more likely that you will retain the information.

Reading this book will save you money. It will also help you have a better idea of whether the attorneys you interview know what they are doing, and whether the way they will pursue your divorce fits your goals.

This book will help you achieve your best divorce.

Chapter 1

CHOOSING AN ATTORNEY

HIRING THE ATTORNEY THAT IS RIGHT FOR YOU at the beginning of the case will save you a tremendous amount of time, money, and heartache. The divorce process is hard to navigate, but having the right attorney to guide you through will make it the best that it can be.

First and foremost, you will need to find an attorney that you can talk to and get along with. You might think that it is more important to hire an attorney based on their skill, experience, or even a dominating presence. But, if you find that your attorney is difficult for you to work with, you may find yourself having to hire a new attorney, or you may end up with an outcome in your case that you are unhappy with. If you are having difficulty working with your attorney, you may not feel confident about their ability to handle your case. Changing attorneys may be necessary in certain circumstances, but it will cost you more money because the new attorney will need to catch up on the case. It is better to make sure from the beginning that the attorney you hire is one you can communicate with and who you believe is best qualified to handle your specific case.

How to Find an Attorney

Online

The easiest way to find potential attorneys in your area that handle divorce is to search online. You can search "family law attorney," "divorce attorney," or similar keywords. You will likely get a list of attorneys in your area and some paid ads. You can click on names and websites to learn more about the attorneys. Shockingly, some of the best and most experienced attorneys do not even have websites and may have very little online presence. This may be because they receive so many referrals that they do not need to have an online presence, or they may not see an online presence as being important.

While searching online is the easiest way to find attorneys, it is not necessarily the best way.

Be wary of asking for referrals through social media, especially in Facebook groups. Even if the group has strict rules about keeping posts in the group confidential, often there is no one to enforce this rule. Even if the rule is enforced, the penalty may only be a message asking them to not do it again or, at worst, the person who broke the confidentiality is no longer welcome in the group. I have seen many people post this kind of referral request in a Facebook group for moms in a particular geographic area, and I personally know of at least one instance where a group member immediately sent the post to the spouse of the person who wrote it. The spouse had not previously known that the person who wrote the post was considering divorce. I'm sure it was a terrible way to find out.

Personal Referrals

Asking friends and family if they know of a good divorce attorney can yield great results. Unfortunately, this option is not readily available to you if you do not want anyone to know that you are considering or starting a divorce. Consider asking another professional for a recommendation. Other professionals are less likely to share that information with anyone else and are even sometimes ethically required to maintain client confidentiality. You can ask your doctor, therapist, real estate agent, or financial professional. These professionals often know attorneys and, more importantly, are aware of their reputations. Remember that a recommendation is not a requirement. Do not hire an attorney that you feel is not the best attorney for you just because they came highly recommended.

Bar Associations, State or Local Lists

Bar associations or judicial websites in your local area may have searchable databases of local attorneys in good standing. These listings often have useful information on each attorney such as years in practice, types of law that they practice, contact and website information. Additionally, you may be able to look up whether or not the attorney you are considering has had any professional disciplinary actions brought against them and why.

THE INITIAL CONSULTATION

If you have decided on the divorce model you want, a major factor in choosing an attorney will be whether they practice in the model you are seeking. For more information on divorce models, see chapter 2. Many attorneys will list what kinds of divorces they assist with on their websites. If not, you can call and ask before you set up an appointment. Most attorneys will practice in the traditional model and not necessarily specify it on their webpages, because it tends to be the default model in most places. If you are still undecided, you can seek an initial consultation with an attorney who practices in several different models, and they can help you choose the best model for your specific case.

Some attorneys will give you a free consultation. This is an opportunity to meet the attorney, tell them about the specifics of your situation, and find out what that attorney sees as your best plan of action going forward. Do not expect to get specific legal advice about your case during a free consultation. While the consultation is confidential, you have not yet hired the attorney.

Some attorneys do charge for the consultation. They may charge their full hourly rate or a reduced rate. There could be several very good reasons for this charge. Some people set up multiple consultations in order to cause a conflict, so that the other party will not be able to hire that attorney. Charging for a consultation may help to discourage this. This might be a frequent or infrequent situation depending on your local area.

Another issue is with people setting up consultations and then not showing up. I have found that more people will show up or call to cancel if they have paid for a consultation.

Charging for consultations may indicate that the attorney is confident in the value they bring to the consultation. They may have years of experience, or they may be in demand.

Remember that the attorney you choose will determine how your divorce will go and can continue to have an impact on your life going forward. Do not pass over an attorney because they charge for a consultation if that attorney otherwise seems to be a good fit for you.

Treat the consultation like a job interview. While it may seem intimidating to meet with an attorney, especially if it is your first time seeking an attorney, remember that you are interviewing them. You absolutely can ask the attorney about their experience and qualifications. If the attorney you are meeting with is not expecting these questions, it is likely because, surprisingly, potential clients do not often ask these questions. However, if the attorney seems unhappy about the questions or avoids answering them, this is a red flag.

Once you have discussed the specifics of your case with them, you should also ask the attorney how they would approach your case. Ask the attorney what models of divorce they practice in and what model of divorce they would recommend for your case. They likely have a perspective on how each model will play out in your specific location. Therefore, if you have decided on a particular model and they are suggesting a different model, hear them out. Of course, be aware that they may be recommending that model because it is the model they are comfortable with. Remember that this is not the only attorney in town; you have options.

I have set up a list of questions that you can ask an attorney during a consultation. Choose the ones that are most important to you or that represent what is important in your case. Do not ask all the questions and turn the consultation into an interrogation.

Often, potential clients only ask me questions about the process and do not ask any questions about my qualifications or how I would approach their case. I would like to think it is because my reputation precedes the consultation, but, more likely, the potential clients do not feel like they can ask those questions.

Sometimes potential clients feel more comfortable bringing a friend or relative to the consultation. Note that bringing a third party with you may make the consultation less confidential because the third party could become a witness in the case.

You are also being interviewed by the attorney. The attorney will ask you questions about your case such as whether you have children, what kind of assets you and your spouse have, whether your spouse has hired an attorney, what issues are likely to be agreed on and what things will likely be contested. If your spouse has already filed for divorce, the attorney will ask you when it was filed, whether you have been served and when, and what your case number is. Be prepared to give them specific information.

They will also be paying close attention to how you talk about your case. Unlike a job interview, keep in mind that you are not trying to get hired and you may not be able to predict what information the attorney is looking for with their questions. Do not try to tell the attorney what you think they want to hear or hide aspects of your case that you think will make the attorney not want to work with you or charge you more. If you are hiding information from the potential attorney, you will not be getting good information from them about what to expect or how much the divorce will cost. When you decide to hire an attorney, you will want them to be a good fit for you and you want to be a good fit for the attorney. If you withhold information, neither of you will truly know if it is a good fit, and you may end up in a working relationship that is not beneficial for either of you. It could damage your case, or you might put yourself in the position of having to hire a new attorney in the middle of your divorce.

At the end of the consultation, some attorneys will tell you whether they will take your case and what the fee options are. Other attorneys might say they will send you that information in a letter or email. If the attorney has decided they will not take your case, they may tell you that in person and give you referrals. Do not take this personally, because their decision may have nothing to do with you. For instance, there might be particular types of cases that they don't take. Or they may not want to work with the attorney who has been hired by the other party. Or they may not take cases in the particular courthouse where your case would need to be brought. Or they may have realized a conflict during the consultation that they cannot discuss. Or it may be as simple as knowing that they are not the best attorney for your case. Do consider the recommendations they have given you, because they might know that the attorney they have recommended would be a good fit.

10 Questions to Ask a Potential Attorney

I have put together a list of questions you may want to ask a potential attorney during an initial consultation. You may be able to learn the answers to some of these questions by reviewing information about the attorney online. Remember that you will have a limited amount of time, so anything you can find out about the attorney prior to the meeting will help you use your time effectively and narrow your list of questions.

When people come to an initial consultation with me, they usually have so many questions about the divorce itself that they do not ask many questions about my experience, qualifications, or even my fee structure or preferred models of practice. The following questions will help you determine if a potential attorney is a good fit for you.

1. **How long have you been practicing family law?** In my opinion this question is more important than how long the attorney has been practicing law. You might be considering an attorney who advertises having ten years of experience, but then you find out they only started practicing family law in the last year. On the other hand, you might

meet with an attorney who has five years of experience but has been practicing family law for all five of those years. This does not mean you cannot hire an attorney with relatively little family law experience. They can tell you why you should hire them if they don't have that experience. They may tell you that, while they have less family law experience, they have mentor attorneys who have been practicing family law for decades. Be aware that litigation or trial experience in another area may not be a good selling point, because trials in family law are very different than other areas of law and only a small percent of family law cases go to trial. Additionally, if you want a more amicable divorce model and the majority of the experience the attorney has is in litigation, they may have a trial preparation approach to your case. However, if you think your case is likely to go to trial, you may want an attorney with more trial experience.

2. **How much of your practice is devoted to family law and what other areas do you practice in?** Some attorneys may have decades of family law experience, but family law only makes up about ten percent of their cases. Other attorneys may specialize in family law almost exclusively.

3. **Are you in good standing with the bar?** There may be a way for you to look this up in your state so you do not have to ask this question during the consultation. If you have looked it up and the attorney does have a disciplinary or ethics violation, but you have chosen to meet with that attorney anyway, you can ask them about the violation and what they have done to address whatever issues caused it. Violations can range from missing deadlines to misusing client funds. Violations can also be based on something that happened in that attorney's personal life rather than anything to do with their legal practice.

4. **Where did you go to law school?** If the attorney went to law school in the same state or even the local area where your case will be filed, that

may give the attorney additional experience in that location. If they did not go to law school locally, you can ask how long they have been practicing in the local area.

5. **Do you have any additional experience, qualifications, or certifications that would be relevant to my specific case?** They may have additional qualifications that are particularly suited to your case, and those qualifications may distinguish them from other attorneys you are considering. This is especially important if you want to use a particular model of divorce, because you will want to know if they have experience, qualifications, or certifications in that model. For example, if you or your spouse have complicated financial assets, it would be helpful to know if the potential attorney has additional qualifications or experience with complicated financial matters.

6. **If I hire you, will you be the attorney primarily working on my case?** In a bigger firm, the attorney you meet with might not be the attorney who works on your case day to day. The attorney may be the main attorney assigned to your case, but the firm may take a team approach. You can ask what their level of involvement in your case will be. The team approach, especially if it includes younger attorneys and paralegals doing some of the work, may be a cost savings to you.

7. **How will you keep me updated on my case?** It is important you know how regular communication is handled or if there is a communication plan. You will want to know if the attorney will update you regularly, if the attorney will only update you if something specific happens, or if you will have to ask for updates. Some attorneys may have a paralegal or other support staff update you and answer your questions. This could save you money if the paralegal is billed at a lower rate. You may decide that you want an attorney who personally handles client communication even if that might be more expensive, or you may be

relieved to know that you can ask a paralegal or other support staff questions when needed.

8. **What is your fee structure and billing practice?** You will want to get the specifics about how the attorney bills before deciding to hire them. If the attorney charges hourly fees, you should ask them if they have a minimum billable hour. You may also want to know how often you will receive an invoice. If you are asked to pay a retainer, you will want to know how often you will receive an update on your trust account balance and when the trust amount will need to be replenished. If the attorney charges a flat fee, you will want to know exactly what is included in the flat fee, what other services you may need that are not included, and how much those additional services cost.

9. **What should I know about you?** This is a nicer way of asking the attorney why you should hire them. The attorney can tell you anything about themselves or their experience that was not already covered in the consultation and may help you make your decision.

10. **What would be your approach to my case?** This is a very important question to ask all the potential attorneys you consult with. The answer to this question should show you whether the attorney's approach to your case will be in line with your goals. This question should be asked toward the end of the consultation, when you have already discussed your goals with the attorney. In that way, it will also show you how much the attorney paid attention to what you had to say during the consultation.

Chapter 2

Divorce Models

THIS CHAPTER WILL SUMMARIZE several divorce models. There may be additional options, not listed here, that are available in your state or local area. The important thing to take away from this chapter is that you have choices.

Many people who are contemplating divorce are not aware that there are different divorce models to choose from. If you don't know what the potential options are, you may unknowingly limit your choices. If the attorney you consult practices exclusively in the traditional model, for example, they are not likely to explain your other options to you. Without this book, you may leave that attorney's office believing that the traditional model is the only choice. Reading this section will give you an understanding of the different available models so you can choose the one that will work best for you and your family. You can then consult with attorneys who practice those divorce models.

TRADITIONAL DIVORCE

Traditional divorce is, even at its best, an adversarial process. While most states have eliminated the need to prove fault in divorce, traditional divorce follows a civil lawsuit model, meaning that one side is suing the other for divorce, the same way you would sue another person or entity for a breach of contract.

Traditional divorce starts with one side filing a Petition (or suit) and will proceed through most of the steps outlined in Chapter 6. The traditional divorce plans for a trial from the beginning, rather than planning for resolution. Most state divorce laws are based on and facilitate a traditional model of divorce. Fortunately, many states are starting to adopt rules and laws that facilitate other models. One incentive for this change is a recognition that traditional divorce is not accessible for many people because of high legal fees – retainers and hourly rates. Additionally, the traditional divorce model tends to clog the court system with trials.

At its worst, traditional divorce can cause more conflict and problems than it resolves. Attorneys in a traditional model of divorce have little incentive to resolve the matter peacefully. The pay structure in a divorce, usually hourly with a large retainer, means the attorney will make less money if they resolve conflict and more money as the conflict in your case continues or worsens.

On the other hand, the traditional model may be your best choice if the other side is not willing to resolve conflict. In that case you may need the traditional model to protect your rights.

Some attorneys may practice primarily in the traditional model but try more cooperative methods until they are no longer effective or until you have an agreement. This might mean a cooperative exchange of needed information instead of discovery, and informal settlement conferences. When you interview an attorney, you can ask them how they would approach your case.

Collaborative Divorce

Collaborative divorce differs in one major aspect from traditional divorce. The parties agree at the beginning of the process that they will not go to trial. This means that steps which are taken purely for trial preparation in a case are no longer needed. Instead of discovery, the parties agree to exchange whatever documents are needed to support the agreement process. Other professionals (see chapter 12) can be brought in to help the parties resolve more complicated matters, and the parties can share in the cost of experts to determine key issues like the valuation of property or a business. In an official collaborative divorce, both attorneys are trained in the collaborative process and usually have also been trained as mediators. If either party defaults on the agreement not to go to trial, both parties will have to obtain new attorneys to begin the trial preparation process.

Cooperative Divorce

Cooperative divorce is similar to collaborative divorce in that the parties agree that they want to settle their divorce as peacefully as possible. The main difference is in cooperative divorce, the parties do not make an agreement not to go to trial. If the case does go to trial, each party's attorney can continue to represent them.

Mediation-First Divorce

You can choose to attend mediation with the other party before involving attorneys or filing for divorce. Depending on who you choose, you may have a mediator who is an attorney, or one who is not an attorney. If the mediator is an attorney, it is important to note that, in the role of mediator, they cannot give either party specific legal advice. If you come to an agreement in mediation, you can hire an attorney to file the necessary paperwork or you can file it yourself if you do not want to hire an attorney. As in the kitchen table divorce model (see below), if your state does not allow one attorney to represent both parties, you may need one attorney to write and file the documents on behalf of one party and another to advise the other party.

Kitchen Table Divorce

A kitchen table divorce might vary depending on the laws of the state where you live. Basically, the idea is that both parties come together at the kitchen table (although of course this discussion could really be anywhere) and work out the terms of their divorce. Then an attorney files the necessary paperwork.

The major difference between a kitchen table divorce and collaborative, cooperative, or mediation-first divorce is that the parties come to an agreement without the help of a mediator or attorney. Then, once they are agreed on all issues, they can proceed through the court process as an uncontested divorce.

In some states, one attorney can represent both parties in an uncontested divorce. In those states, the attorney might be at the "kitchen table" with the parties, possibly even drafting the documents on the spot. In states that do not allow one attorney to represent both parties, the parties would need to come to an agreement on their own and then one party would hire an attorney to draw up the necessary paperwork. The other party could hire an attorney just to review the paperwork or that party could represent themselves. This model of divorce can be very cost effective if the divorce is amicable.

Chapter 3

Fee Structures

Hourly

AN HOURLY RATE IS THE MOST WIDELY USED payment structure. An attorney will set an hourly rate that usually depends on experience and location. The attorney will then estimate how much time your case will take and give you the amount they will require you to pay up front. This upfront fee is usually called a retainer, because it is the amount of money you need in order to retain (or keep) the services of the attorney.

Typically, attorneys charge by the tenth of the hour. For instance, if you call your attorney and talk to them for twelve minutes, you will likely be charged two tenths of an hour (.2). Your retainer agreement should specify whether the charges are rounded down or rounded up to the nearest tenth of an hour. If you talk to that attorney for 13 minutes, will you still be charged for two tenths of an hour (.2) or will they round up to three tenths (.3)?

The agreement should also specify whether there is a minimum charge. Some attorneys charge a minimum of two tenths of an hour (or more) for everything they do on your case. The reasoning for this is that even if your case has diverted their attention for only a couple of minutes, they should be paid for a segment of time because of having to transition from what they were doing to your case and back.

This billable event may be something you have initiated by calling or emailing your attorney, or it may be initiated by things beyond your control, such as the other party's attorney calling or emailing your attorney, the court calling your attorney, or your attorney receiving a filing or order that they must review.

If your fee agreement with your attorney is based on an hourly rate, you will want to consider the best way for you to initiate a billable event. If you email or call your attorney every time you have a question, thought, or information about your case, the fees can quickly add up – especially if your attorney rounds up and has a minimum hourly charge.

I would not suggest withholding your questions, thoughts, or information from your attorney. However, you can save a lot of money if you write things down throughout the day and send them to your attorney all at one time. You can also keep a record of your questions, thoughts, and information and then make an appointment to discuss them with your attorney by phone or in person. I have had clients who email me every day to ask what is going on in their case. This costs them $30 or more per day and it does not give them much value for their money.

Suppose you have a question about what to expect at an upcoming hearing. You want to avoid paying for a half hour phone appointment, so you email your attorney. Your attorney emails you back an answer, but the answer gives rise to another question. So you email that question, and the attorney emails you back. Later in the day you realize you forgot to ask how early you should be for the hearing, so you email your attorney again, and the attorney emails back. You may have just racked up anywhere from .6 to 1.2 billable hours, depending on your attorney's billing policy. In contrast, you could have scheduled a half-hour appointment by phone with your attorney and discussed everything at once. You will likely save money and will have an uninterrupted half hour of your attorney's time. Additionally, you most likely will get more information, have all your questions answered at once, and be able to ask for any necessary clarifications.

Flat Fee

Some attorneys offer flat fee options. This may also be called a fixed fee. The total fee will be based on the estimate of time the attorney believes the case will take multiplied by the hourly rate of the attorney.

While this sounds similar to a retainer in the hourly fee structure, with flat fees you will not pay anything additional if your divorce takes longer. However, you are also not likely to get a refund if your divorce takes less time, depending on the attorney's policy.

The benefit of the flat fee option is that you can have more certainty about what your divorce is going to cost. You will not have to worry about racking up a bill by emailing or calling your attorney too much, which may result in better communication with your attorney. Some attorneys may put a limit on emails, phone calls, or total excess attorney time. Even with restrictions, however, a flat-fee arrangement can provide better communication between you and your attorney, because you will know exactly how much of your attorney's time you have, and you can plan accordingly. Some attorneys who offer flat fees may set up regular communication appointments by phone or in person. This way you always have a set time to discuss any issues and questions you have, and you will have a better understanding of the timeline. Having a planned out, no surprises approach to your divorce can reduce your anxiety with the process.

Make sure you know exactly what the flat fee covers, because some attorneys price the flat fee to include only the services the attorney thinks you will need in your divorce. Often the initial flat fee will not include a trial, so if you find you do have to go to trial, the attorney may have an additional flat fee for trial services or may charge you hourly from that point forward. Ask the attorney how a trial will be handled. You may be able to add other services as needed, like discovery or mediation, but they will likely be at an additional cost.

Unbundled Services

Unbundled services are similar to flat fees but, instead of having one flat fee for the entirety of the services you might need, each individual service can be specifically priced. With this fee structure you can pick what services you need and what parts of your divorce you will handle yourself. If legal fees were listed on a menu like in a restaurant, unbundled services would be listed under sides or a la carte. An example of unbundled services would be the following:

- Draft and file Petition.
- Represent client in a temporary matters hearing.
- Calculate spousal or child support.
- Assist client in answering discovery request.
- Draft and file agreement.
- Represent client for mediation.
- Prepare and file QDRO.
- Draft quitclaim.

Monthly Fee/Subscription Model

This fee structure is new and not widely used as yet. In some models this could be very similar to a flat fee that is broken up over the time the attorney thinks it will take to finish your divorce. For instance, if the flat fee is $6,000 and the attorney believes the divorce will be finished in six months, your monthly fee would be $1,000.

Other subscription models might be based on the client doing most of the work and having monthly access to resources through the law firm, like educational material, forms, a paralegal, software, and perhaps a certain amount of time with an attorney per month. While the time you get with an attorney sounds like an unbundled service, the attorney's time would be used to assist you rather than do any of the work for you. You would be filling out your own forms, filing with the court, keeping track of court hearings and deadlines, and appearing in court by yourself when necessary.

Because this model is so new, there will be many variations. If your attorney offers this fee structure, make sure you know exactly what is included, how many months you are committing to pay for, and what will happen if you no longer want to be a client. Find out what will happen if your divorce takes longer, or if you need to go to trial.

Chapter 4

REPRESENTING YOURSELF

AFTER CONSIDERING HIRING AN ATTORNEY, divorce models, and fee structures, you may think you would rather just represent yourself. Representing yourself is also called being *pro se,* meaning for yourself. Your local rules might be different if you or the other party are *pro se.*

While some people represent themselves because they cannot afford an attorney, others choose to represent themselves to save money on attorney fees. If you are not able to afford attorney fees, I have suggestions on how you may be able to get assistance; check the frequently asked questions section in chapter 14. If you are trying to save money, please proceed with caution. If you do not understand what you are doing or do not have resources to help you, you may make mistakes that will ultimately cost you more than the attorney fees you save.

If you decide to represent yourself, you can hire an attorney for specific parts of your divorce—for instance, to help you prepare documents or to represent you in a specific hearing. You can also hire an attorney to coach you through representing yourself. For more information refer to unbundled services in chapter 3. You may also want to hire some of the other professionals described in chapter 12. You can determine what you are comfortable doing on your own and pay for representation only for the parts of the case where you need help. This can be a cost-effective way to benefit from the assistance of an attorney and reduce the chances of costly mistakes while remaining mostly *pro se*.

However, if there is an attorney representing the other party, you need to be clear about what your status is. If you act as though you have an attorney by making statements like, "Send over the document and I will have my attorney review it," you might find that the attorney stops communicating with you. This is because, ethically, the other party's attorney cannot discuss legal matters directly with you if you are also represented by an attorney.

Your state may have resources online that can assist you in representing yourself. Search for a state judicial or justice department website. You may be able to find resources that have specific information for the public about self-representation, including instructions and forms you can use. Some states, nonprofits, and for-profit organizations have software programs you can use to create your petition and other documents. Make sure that the forms you are using or creating online will be accepted by your local court. If you are having trouble finding state specific materials online, you can try calling your local courthouse, local nonprofit organizations such as Legal Aid, or your local bar association.

Chapter 5

CHILDREN AND DIVORCE

THERE IS SO MUCH INFORMATION to cover when it comes to Children and Divorce that it needs its own book. This chapter is intended to be a brief overview of divorce where minor children are involved, including potential issues and additional steps to consider. If minor children were born during the marriage, the estimated time and cost of the divorce will increase. In a divorce without children, the main issues are property division, spousal support, attorney fees and costs. When minor children are involved, the additional issues are custody, child support, and attorney or *guardian ad litem* fees for the child.

Less frequently, there may be issues regarding paternity or even maternity, meaning who the biological parents of the children are. Most states presume that any children born or conceived during the marriage are legally the children of the marital couple, even if that is not the biological reality. If the parties want to dispute or overcome that presumption, they will have to take additional steps.

A child may also need their own attorney or a *guardian ad litem*, or possibly both An attorney for a child is the same as an attorney for an adult; they represent what the child wants. A *guardian ad litem* represents what is in the best interests of the child. Even though the word "guardian" is in the title, a *guardian ad litem* is not making decisions for or about the child. The *guardian ad litem* will be presenting a position to the court on what will serve the child's best interests.

Usually, an attorney is more appropriate for an older child, while a *guardian ad litem* is more appropriate for a younger child who may not be able to form or verbalize their own preferences. Sometimes a child may have both an attorney and a *guardian ad litem*.

If you have an attorney, they will likely be able to recommend an attorney or *guardian ad litem* for the child. If you are representing yourself or if the parties cannot agree on an attorney or *guardian ad litem*, the court may appoint one.

Custody can be a major point of contention. There are two major types of custody, legal custody and physical custody. Legal custody concerns decisions about the children in areas such as religion, medical care, school, and extracurricular activities. Usually both parents share in the legal custody decisions, unless a court finds the parents are unable to do so. Physical custody concerns who the children are living with. If the children are living primarily with one parent, that parent is the primary physical custodian. The other parent might have parenting time or visitation specified in the final decree. The parties might share physical custody, which means that each parent has as close to equal parenting time as possible.

Together with the day-to-day custody arrangement, there are other custody decisions to make. For instance, the parents will need to decide what will happen for holidays and birthdays. Some families might share holidays while others might alternate holidays. Parents will also have to determine what holidays are important to them and how those holidays are defined. For example, some families might not celebrate Halloween at all, while for other families it might be an important holiday. For families that celebrate Christmas, some might define Christmas as being primarily Christmas Day while other families might celebrate most of the holiday on Christmas Eve. Summer vacation may need a different parenting schedule than the school year does, and parents may want to have an extended period of time so they can take the child on vacation. There may be other issues to work out regarding things like transportation, extracurricular activities, and family events.

The next major issue is child support. Child support depends on the custody arrangement. If one parent is the primary physical custodian, then the other party will pay child support. If both parents have shared physical custody, the parent who makes more money may still pay some child support to the other parent. The parent ordered to pay child support may feel insulted because they think the court is implying that they won't take care of their children financially unless ordered to do so. Unfortunately, some parents will not take care of their children financially unless ordered to do so. The court is looking out for the child and also looking out for the state because, if the parents are not financially supporting their children when they are able to do so, it usually falls to the state to fill the gaps with various forms of welfare.

Another point of contention may be that the amount of support is too high for the parent who is paying it, or not enough to meet the expenses of the child. After a divorce, most of the expenses of the marital home are doubled. The income of both parties will have to stretch further. There will be two homes, with two house payments and two sets of utility bills. The expenses for the children will also increase, because now there needs to be provisions for the child in each home. Some things can be transported, but it would be unreasonable to expect a child to carry everything they need with them from one parent's home to the other.

Most states use an income shares model to calculate child support. This means that child support is calculated based on the combined income of the parties and the percentage of that income that a typical couple would spend per year on their children. One party may complain that the other party is not working or not working enough. Most states allow the income that the party should be making to be considered in the calculation, especially if the underemployment was caused or chosen by that party.

The calculation is complicated. Reduction of income by one party may not actually increase the child support that parent would receive, because it may lower the household's overall bracket. In that case, it will reduce the overall support that is available to the child from both parties.

Here is an example. Mindy and Josh live in Iowa and have a combined net income of $100,000. According to the child support guidelines in Iowa, a family with one child and $100,000 in income spend an average of $1,388 to support that child. Mindy makes $60,000 and Josh makes $40,000 of the combined $100,000. Mindy and Josh are still trying to decide what the custody arrangement will be. If Mindy and Josh decide that shared care will be best for the child and each of them have the child fifty percent of the time, child support will be calculated first as if Mindy has primary physical custody and again as if Josh has primary physical custody. The results of these two calculations will be offset (the smaller amount subtracted from the larger amount) and the person who would pay the higher amount will now pay the offset amount (the difference between the two numbers). In this example Mindy will likely pay some child support to Josh. However, Josh travels a lot for work, so they are considering it might be best for Mindy to have primary custody of the child. In that case, the guidelines will assume that Mindy is contributing her sixty percent of financial support directly to the children. What she is paying directly will be disproportionate, because she will also be responsible for supplying the children with all their primary care needs (food, clothes, extracurricular expenses, etc.). Therefore, Josh will be ordered to pay his forty percent to Mindy. There are other considerations in the child support calculations that could increase or decrease the amount that either party pays, such as who is providing health insurance for the children or other expenses such as daycare.

Of course, this example is a very simplified overview. In every state there are specific rules about how to calculate child support, what counts as net income, what should be subtracted from income, how to handle additional expenses, and when it is appropriate for the court to vary from the guideline amount.

For additional information about the issues of divorce involving minor children, see *Where to Start: Children and Divorce.*

Chapter 6

THE DIVORCE PROCESS - AN OVERVIEW

When I first meet with potential clients, they usually have no idea what the divorce process entails. If they do have an idea of what the process is like, it is usually because they have been divorced before, have witnessed a friend or family member going through divorce, or have had consultations with other attorneys. The following overview will give you confidence in making decisions about what model of divorce you want, what fee structure is going to work best for you, and what kind of attorney you want to hire. After the summary overview, we will take up each section of the divorce process in more detail.

The divorce process has four main stages: beginning, middle, end, and post-decree. Your divorce might have a slightly different order, depending on your jurisdiction, the model of divorce you choose, and your attorney. For instance, if you have chosen a collaborative divorce, you might start with a collaborative meeting before anything is filed with the court. To some extent, once a divorce is filed, the court will set deadlines to keep the process moving forward.

THE DIVORCE ROADMAP
An overview

1 ▸ **2** ▸

BEGINNING STAGE

This stage may take anywhere from one to two months and will include things like filing or answering the petition, assets preservation, and more.

MIDDLE STAGE

This stage includes things like classes, mediation, and hearings that may or may not be court ordered but are all aimed at settling the case. This stage may take three to four months. It may feel like things are moving slowly during this stage.

3

END STAGE

The end stage of the divorce process will proceed down one of two roads, either stipulation (agreement) or trial. This can take a month or over a year depending on which road you take.

4

AFTER STAGE

You or your former spouse may have post-decree requirements that need to be completed, the most common are transferring ownership of property, refinancing, and dividing retirements funds.

Overview

Once you have decided to move forward with a divorce, or if you have been served with a divorce petition, you will be entering the beginning stage of the divorce process. The **beginning stage** may take anywhere from one to two months and will include some of the following:

- Filing or Answering the Petition
- Process Service or Acceptance of Service
- Gathering, Sharing, Creating, and Filing Documents
- Temporary Matters Hearing
- Appointment of a *Guardian ad Litem* (if minor children are involved)
- Assets Preservation

The middle stage of the divorce takes some time, and it may feel like not a lot is happening. If your state requires a waiting period between filing the divorce and finalizing the divorce, the middle stage will partly consist of waiting out the time requirement. The **middle stage** might take three to four months and may include some or all of the following:

- Required Classes
- Conciliation Efforts
- Pretrial Conference
- Settlement Attempts
- Mediation or Settlement Conference
- Trial Scheduling Conference
- Discovery
- Status Conference

The end stage of the divorce process will proceed down one of two roads, either stipulation (agreement) or trial. Both roads will get you to your destination: the filing of a Final Decree which will be the official end of the marriage. If you can come to an agreement and file a stipulation, the end stage may take less than a month. However, if you are going to trial, the **end stage** can take up to a year or even more, depending on your jurisdiction and the issues in your case.

- Agreement , or
- Trial Preparation and Trial
- Final Decree

Lastly, in the post-decree stage of your divorce, you or your former spouse may have post-decree requirements that need to be completed to comply with the final decree, the most common are transferring ownership of property and refinancing property. Also, either party may seek changes in the decree. Typically, you will have thirty days to complete your post-decree requirements. Appeals will have specific deadlines. Modifications can happen years later, but only under specific circumstances. The **post-decree stage** may include some or all of the following:

- Post-trial Requirements
- Appeal
- Modification

Chapter 7

THE DIVORCE PROCESS - BEGINNING STAGE

Filing or Answering the Petition and Process Service

IN MOST DIVORCE MODELS, the process begins with one side, called the "Petitioner," filing a petition for divorce. Either party can become the Petitioner by filing the petition. In Iowa this filing is called a Petition for Dissolution of Marriage, but the title of this document may vary depending on your state.

The court will then approve or reject the filing. The filing can be rejected if the information is not complete or there is a defect in the documents filed. If this happens, the petition will have to be corrected and filed again. It may take some time for the court to approve the filing. This could be because the court has many other filings ahead of yours.

During the approval process, the court may also issue an order or other information regarding the responsibilities of each party to the case, including how the case will proceed, hearing dates, and deadlines. The Petitioner is then responsible for serving the petition and any other documents required by the court on their spouse. The spouse is then called the Respondent. You and your spouse may also be referred to as a "party" or "the parties." You may also hear yourself or your spouse referred to as "the opposing party." These are all shorthand for saying "a party to the case."

The process of serving the Respondent is called "process service." There can be significant delays here if the Respondent evades service or cannot be found. In that case, there are other methods of service you can try, but often you will have to seek permission of the court to do so. Such difficulties in process service are the exception and not the rule.

Once the Respondent is served, they will have a specific amount of time to file an Answer to the Petition.

In other divorce models, your divorce might begin with mediation or with meetings to decide on all the issues of your divorce before filing. In these models, filing may be the last thing that happens.

Gathering, Sharing, Creating, and Filing Documents

Both parties may be required to exchange certain documents at the beginning of the case. Required documents may include:

- Tax returns
- Paycheck stubs
- W2s
- Financial affidavit
- Child support guidelines

You may not need to exchange these files if your spouse already has a copy or access to these documents.

The financial affidavit is a statement of your assets, debts, income, and expenses; it is a document that will have to be created by you or an attorney. If there are children who were born or adopted during the marriage who will require support, the parties may also be required to create and file a document that shows who they believe should pay child support and what amount it should be. If either party is asking for spousal support (also called alimony), the parties may be required to submit a document that shows what amount they believe the spousal support should be.

In the preparation of these documents, you will likely need to gather other important financial information. Some courts require that you exchange all documents that you have used in the preparation of your filings. For example, if you put on your financial affidavit that you have a car loan with an outstanding balance of $8,000, the court may require you to provide the most recent loan statement to the other party if they do not already have access to it.

Temporary Matters Hearing, Guardian ad Litem, and Assets Preservation

Either party can file a motion requesting a temporary matters hearing. This type of hearing may also be referred to as a Hearing *Pendente Lite*. The literal translation of *Pendente Lite* is "pending litigation." In other words, a Hearing *Pendente Lite* would be a hearing to determine matters temporarily while awaiting trial or a final agreement.

A temporary matters hearing may be necessary to determine issues like child custody, child support and spousal support while the divorce is pending. Together with the temporary matters hearing or separately, either party can also file a motion requesting the court to appoint a *guardian ad litem* or attorney for the children, or to issue an order to preserve assets. In some states, the court will automatically issue an order to preserve assets. The parties may be required to attend mediation or a settlement conference to attempt to work out these temporary matters on their own before they have a hearing on these requests. Any agreement or order that results from these motions will then be in place until a final decree is entered in the divorce, unless they are modified by the court before the final decree is entered.

Chapter 8

THE DIVORCE PROCESS - MIDDLE STAGE

THE ORDER OF EVENTS AND REQUIREMENTS will vary by state laws and by the model of divorce you have selected. During the middle stage, you will either be working towards a final agreement or preparing for a trial. Sometimes both avenues are pursued at the same time.

PRETRIAL CONFERENCE

The court may set a date for a Pretrial Conference at the beginning of the case. The purpose of the Pretrial Conference, depending on your state, may be to make sure all parties have complied with the pre-trial requirements of the court, and the court likely wants to know what issues remain outstanding in the case, meaning what issues the parties are not able to agree on. Your state may have additional requirements for the Pretrial Conference.

Instead of attending a Pretrial Conference, the court may allow the parties to file an affidavit or certificate stating that they have complied with all the preliminary requirements of the court and stating what issues are outstanding. If the parties have not fulfilled the requirements, or if one or more parties are representing themselves, the court may require the parties to attend the

Pretrial Conference. If you have an attorney, they can let you know whether you will have to attend a Pretrial Conference. In some states the Pretrial Conference may be called a Status Conference.

Required Classes

If you and your spouse have children, you may both be required to take a class commonly called Children in the Middle or Children in Between. The class is intended to help divorcing parents learn how to minimize the impact of divorce on their children and prevent them from putting their children in the middle of any ongoing conflict. Most of my clients have found the class to be helpful.

Depending on the rules where your divorce is filed, there may be other classes that you, your spouse, or your children are required to take. For instance, some counties in Iowa now require parents to enroll their children in a workshop aimed at helping them through the divorce. Any class you are required to attend should give you a certificate or other proof that you attended. That certificate will need to be filed with the court as part of your pre-trial requirements.

Conciliation

Some state divorce laws require a period of conciliation. Conciliation includes all services related to preserving the marriage. The most common example is marriage counseling. The court may specify how long the parties must engage in conciliation efforts and which party will be responsible for initiating conciliation. In some states the conciliation requirement may be waived if both parties believe that conciliation will not be beneficial.

Settlement Attempts

During this part of the process either party may propose a final or temporary agreement to the other party. Any time the parties reach a full agreement on all issues in the divorce, that agreement can be signed by both parties and filed with the court. If the agreement is approved by the court, a final order or decree will be filed, and your divorce will be final. There are clear benefits to resolving your case in this way, because you will not have to go through the time, money, and stress of the following stages.

Mediation or Settlement Conference

Mediation might be required by the court before you can set a trial date. If you have attempted mediation already and have not reached an agreement, this attempt might be sufficient for the court. However, if the previous mediation was required for a different specific purpose (such as a mediation required before a temporary matters hearing), you may be required to mediate again specifically for final resolution of the case. Some states may not require mediation.

Other states might require a settlement conference instead. A settlement conference is an opportunity for the parties to resolve any issues they can prior to trial. The discussion and result of a settlement conference may be very similar to a mediation but without a mediator present.

Trial Scheduling Conference

If an agreement is not reached in mediation or settlement conference, the parties will be required to attend a trial scheduling conference. If you are represented by an attorney, you may not be required to be present as your attorney will attend for you. The trial dates will be set at the trial scheduling conference. The trial scheduling conference is also the time to determine the approximate number of days the parties expect to need for the trial and to set deadlines regarding discovery, depositions, and experts.

Discovery

Discovery is the process used by the parties to ask each other for information in preparation for trial. Depending on the divorce model you use, discovery may be formal or informal.

In an informal discovery process, the parties agree to freely exchange information needed to work towards an agreement. For example, if you need to know the current balance of the other party's 401k, your attorney can just ask the other party's attorney for a copy of the latest statement. Informal discovery can occur in a traditional divorce model. However, at the point where it becomes likely that a trial will be necessary, the parties should switch to a more formal process, because informal discovery cannot be enforced or disputed in court.

There are three types of formal discovery requests: Requests for Production of Documents, Requests for Admissions, and Interrogatories.

Requests for Production of Documents are a list of documents in one party's possession that the other side wants an opportunity to see, inspect, or receive a copy of.

Requests for Admissions are a list of statements that a party is asked to either deny or admit. Depending on your state laws, a failure to respond to a Request for Admissions may result in the court viewing those statements as admitted.

Interrogatories are questions that one party is requesting that the other party answer in writing. Usually, Interrogatories include a request that a copy of any documents supporting the answers be provided to the requesting party.

The discovery process can also include depositions, subpoenas, and examinations of mental and physical health. There are many rules about discovery, including what can be asked, how many questions and requests can be made, how much time each party will be given to respond, and when the discovery process must be completed.

The rules of discovery are not just for divorce; your state may have the same rules for many kinds of cases. Your state may also have specific discovery rules for divorce.

If you receive a discovery request, your attorney should review the request with you and help you determine which documents you will need to provide, which questions are appropriate to answer and what requests can be objected to. How much your attorney helps you with this process will depend on your attorney. If you do not have an attorney and you are served with discovery, it will be well worth the money to hire an attorney to go over the discovery requests with you.

The discovery process is time consuming and expensive. There might be a great deal of back and forth between the attorneys on discovery issues. For example, your attorney may object to certain discovery requests, the opposing attorney may disagree with that objection and may seek a ruling on the issue from the court. This disagreement might be brought to the attention of the court in a pleading called a Motion to Compel, and the court may set a hearing on the motion. Some courts may have rules on what attorneys will be required to do to resolve discovery disputes before the court will set a hearing.

In a traditional divorce, both parties are – to some extent – preparing for trial from the beginning. Discovery is a big part of the trial preparation process. It is your attorney's opportunity to discover all the relevant information in preparation for a trial.

Some attorneys believe that all cases require formal discovery, even if the goal is to settle the case without going to trial. If you choose not to have formal discovery, even though you will save money, understand that you might not be getting all the information you need to make a completely informed and fair settlement agreement. If your spouse has a bank account that you are unaware of and they do not disclose it during the divorce, that asset will not be taken into account in the settlement.

If your state requires a financial affidavit or some other kind of financial disclosure, there may be penalties for not disclosing major assets. Keeping a bank account secret, for instance, may be a reason for the court to set aside the final decree. Or the court may be able to modify the decree later to address that asset. However, even if there is a remedy for a party's failure to disclose, it is better to have all the information you both need to have a final and fair resolution.

While your attorney knows the law, you know your marriage and your spouse better than your attorney does. If both you and your spouse worked together on the family finances, you may have equal access to the information you need, and discovery may not be necessary. However, if your spouse has been in control of the finances and you do not have access to that information, you may need at least some informal or formal discovery.

Status Conference

There will likely be another hearing or conference between discovery and the trial. This will be an opportunity for the attorneys to discuss trial-related issues. For example, the attorneys may agree in advance on what exhibits they will not object to. These conferences are meant to save time, money, and judge irritation. The attorneys may use this time to settle any outstanding discovery issues. The status conference is also a last-minute opportunity to settle the case or identify issues that are no longer contested and do not need to be addressed by the court.

Sometimes the discovery process can lead to an agreement because all the information is now accessible to both sides and the likely outcome of a trial may be clearer than it was at the beginning of the case. Your attorney should advise you on the merits of settlement versus trial. If there is still no agreement on all issues after the status conference, your next step will be trial.

Chapter 9

THE DIVORCE PROCESS - END STAGE

Agreement

YOU MAY HAVE REACHED AN AGREEMENT on all or part of the issues in your case. One party will need to put the agreement in writing in a format that the court will accept. If either you or the other party have an attorney, the attorney will put the agreement in writing. If neither party has an attorney, you can hire an attorney just to write the agreement, or you may be able to find acceptable forms at your courthouse or your state's judicial branch website and fill them out yourself. For more options, see chapter 4 on representing yourself.

Once the agreement is in writing, it will be filed with the court. If you have not agreed on all issues, the remaining issues will be resolved in trial.

Trial Preparation

In courtroom dramas you frequently see an attorney ask a question and everyone in the courtroom is shocked by the answer. In reality, preparing for a trial is more like putting on a play for the judge. Well-prepared attorneys will know the answer to every question they ask and will have anticipated most of the questions the other attorney will ask. When there is a surprise, it is usually because a witness has lied, either previously or in the courtroom. In that case, your attorney will be prepared to show that the witness is lying. This level of mastery over your case in trial takes a lot of preparation and can be very expensive.

As the trial date nears, the attorneys should be making and exchanging witness and exhibit lists. Attorneys will list all the witnesses they could possibly need, but they are not likely to call all the potential witnesses to the stand.

Attorneys put extra witnesses on the list for a variety of reasons. Sometimes a witness is on the list so they can be kept out of the courtroom during testimony. For example, an attorney may know that a witness is going to have a hard time testifying in front of a particular person, so the attorney might put that person on the witness list so they will not be in the courtroom.

While your attorney should consult with you regarding who should and who should not be a witness in your case, keep in mind that the more witnesses you have, the longer and more expensive your trial will be. You may have many people who would tell the court what a wonderful person you are or, if you have kids, what a wonderful parent you are. However, this volume of favorable testimony is not going to make as big an impact on the judge as you might think. The judge expects your friends and family to think you are a wonderful person and parent, even if you are not. Your attorney will know which witnesses will have the most positive impact.

As part of trial preparation, your attorney should be preparing you for what to expect during the trial as well as preparing you to testify. Your attorney will go over what questions they intend to ask you and what questions the other attorney will likely ask you. Your attorney should also tell you if there are any local court rules you need to know.

Sometimes your attorney will talk to you about how to present yourself in court. Don't take this personally. If your attorney knows who the judge will be prior to trial, these recommendations will be based on what that judge prefers or what the local rules or customs are.

Trial

Arrive at the courthouse early on the day of trial. This will give you an opportunity to see the courtroom and become familiar with your surroundings.

The judge may start by having a quick meeting with both attorneys in the judge's chambers or in the open courtroom. You may or may not be present for this. If you do not have an attorney, you should be included in this meeting because you are representing yourself.

This meeting will be practical in nature. The judge will likely ask the attorneys (or *pro se* party) what issues still need to be decided, what has been agreed on procedurally, if there any special needs for witnesses or exhibits, and how long the attorneys think they will need for trial. Based on this information, the judge might set a schedule for the day including breaks (also called recesses).

The judge will also go over any additional rules that are not part of the written local court rules. Some local court rules may already specify the order of witnesses in the trial. For example, the rules may state that the Petitioner will testify first, then the Respondent, then the Petitioner's witnesses, and lastly the Respondent's witnesses. If the rules do not specify, the judge will likely make that decision before the trial starts. Any outstanding motions that still need to be ruled on can be brought to the judge's attention at this meeting.

Unless your divorce is in Texas, there will not be a jury deciding your divorce case. One judge will hear your case from beginning to end and will make the final ruling in your case. That judge will also make all the rulings during the trial.

The most frequent ruling the judge will make during the trial is to respond to objections. Either attorney may make objections to the questions asked of a witness, the form of the questions asked, the answer itself, or an exhibit or a particular witness. You may have some familiarity with this if you have served on a jury or if you watch courtroom dramas.

In family law cases there are not as many objections as you would see, for example, in a criminal case. This is because the goals in a family law case are different than those in a criminal case. A judge in a family law case is focused on fairness and on the best interests of any children who are involved. For this reason, evidence that would not be admitted in criminal court can be admitted in family court, if the evidence is likely to assist in those goals. Without knowing this, you might be surprised that your attorney is not making objections left and right.

Your attorney will be strategic about when or if they object. The judge can sustain the objection, which means that whatever is being objected to cannot continue. For example, if the objection is to a question and the judge rules that the objection is sustained, then the witness will not be allowed to answer the question. If the judge states that the objection is overruled, that means whatever is being objected to can continue, i.e., the witness can answer the question. The judge may also ask the attorney to give more information about the objection and may give the opposing attorney an opportunity to argue why the objection should be overruled. Sometimes the attorney who did not make the objection will ask to make an offer of proof, which means the attorney wants the opportunity to show the judge how that question is relevant or important to the case.

After the trial, the judge may ask the attorneys to submit briefs on one or more specific issues. A brief is a summary of the law, how it has been interpreted in other cases (called case law), and how it should be applied to the evidence produced during this trial.

The judge may also direct the attorneys to submit proposed decrees, a draft of what you are asking the judge to order in your case.

The judge might rule from the bench, which means that the judge will tell the parties during the court session what the ruling will be. The judge might then direct one attorney to draft a decree based on those rulings. If there is no ruling from the bench, the judge might then take several weeks, and sometimes even months, to decide your case. The judge may tell you how long to expect, or your attorney may tell you approximately what to expect.

Decree

Your divorce will eventually end with an order from the court dissolving your marriage. This order is called a decree. The judge may approve an agreement or stipulation that you and the other party have signed and filed. In that case, the judge will file a decree adopting your agreement. If there is no agreement, the judge will make decisions on all the outstanding issues in your case. The judge will put the decisions in a decree or order. The decree will be based on what the judge heard and received as evidence during your trial and applicable law.

Chapter 10

THE DIVORCE PROCESS - AFTER THE DIVORCE

AFTER THE FINAL ORDER in your divorce is filed, you are divorced. Whether you wanted the divorce to happen or you didn't, congratulations are still in order because you have made it through the process.

But even after the divorce is final, there are usually still steps which need to be taken.

The final divorce order or decree may have errors, or it may include orders you do not agree with. Discuss what specific options you have with your attorney.

If there are no issues with the decree, there still may be requirements in the order that you will have to complete, usually within a certain amount of time. Your attorney should be able to help you complete these tasks. These tasks might include transferring ownership of property or refinancing a loan. If either party fails to comply with the court order, an Application for an Order to Show Cause (also known as a Contempt) can be filed to enforce the post-decree requirements.

Additionally, modifications may be needed in the years to come regarding things like child support, custody, or spousal support. Usually, property divisions are permanent and cannot be modified.

You Must Read the Final Decree!

I have had clients tell me that when they received the final decree, they put it in a drawer or saved it on their computer and never read it. They have now come to me needing to modify their decree, a step they may have been able to avoid had they thoroughly read the final order when they first received it.

Once your attorney tells you that your divorce is final, you will be eager to move on, and the last thing you will want to do is read through the judge's order or a stipulation. While the decree and stipulation may contain a lot of legalese and can seem daunting, it's important to read it all while you still have an attorney who can walk you through it and answer questions. Not reading it promptly can be a costly mistake, because modifying the decree can cost as much time and money as the original divorce. In most jurisdictions, the property settlement of a divorce cannot be modified at all, so if there is a mistake that awards property incorrectly and you do not address it right away, you may not be able to recover property that was supposed to be yours.

When the judge issues the final Decree or Order, read the entire ruling very carefully and ask your attorney about anything you do not understand or anything that seems wrong to you. If you see a paragraph in a Decree that does not seem to be related to your case or not part of an agreement you made, say something to your attorney. If you don't have an attorney, you may want to hire one to go over the final decree with you.

Keep in mind that any ruling will have parts you agree with and parts that you don't agree with. However, if you substantially disagree with the ruling or if you think something went wrong with the process, talk to your attorney about your specific options. You have more options right after a ruling than you will have later, because some of those options have a time limit.

Post Decree Options

If the mistake is minor – for instance the judge refers to you as "petitioner" when you are "respondent," making the rest of the order confusing – your attorney can file a Motion for a *Nunc Pro Tunc* (translated as now for then). Errors in the order can be changed when it is obvious that it was a mistake or a typo. I once found a whole paragraph in an order that was about the substance abuse issues of one of the parties, yet there had been no evidence to suggest either party had a substance abuse issue.

Attorneys and judges are fond of using previous documents as a basis for new documents. Not only does this keep pleadings and orders consistent, but it is also a great way to save time and money. Believe it or not, most attorneys do try to save their clients time and money. The only downside of using a previous document as a template is that something might be left in the final version that is not relevant to the case.

This is how the substance abuse paragraph erroneously made it into the order, but it was easy to fix with a *Nunc Pro Tunc* since we caught the error right away.

If the issue with the order is a little more than a mistake or typo, your attorney might need to file a Motion to Reconsider. A Motion to Reconsider is exactly what it sounds like, it is a motion that asks the judge to reconsider the order. The motion should also explain specifically why the party believes it needs to be reconsidered.

For instance, suppose the court ordered an amount for child support but used the wrong income for the parties. A *Nunc Pro Tunc* may not be appropriate because, even if the court changes the income numbers to the correct amount, it will not entirely fix the issue. The calculation the judge made to come up with a child support amount will need to be done again with the correct income numbers.

If you disagree with the ruling of the court, your attorney may still want to start with a Motion to Reconsider, because it is more time and cost effective. If the court does not reconsider, your next option is an appeal. For instance, if you asked for primary custody and the court recognized that you asked for primary custody but ruled that the other party should have primary custody instead, you will want to discuss the option of an appeal with your attorney.

The following are examples of how post decree options work.

Jane and Pat went to trial on their divorce. They could not agree on custody because both parties felt that they should have primary custody of their two children. In court, Jane provided evidence that she had been the children's primary caregiver because Pat worked long hours, while Jane worked primarily from home and was available to take the kids to school and pick them up. Jane was usually the parent that set appointments for the kids and took them to those appointments. Jane and Pat both provided evidence of their ability to parent, and the evidence clearly showed that both parents love and care for their children equally but that they just can't get along well enough to share custody. The court issued a final order awarding primary custody to Pat. In the section on child support, the court ordered Jane to pay child support, but then started referring to Jane as Respondent even though Pat is actually the Respondent. Pat's attorney files for a *Nunc Pro Tunc* to make sure there is no confusion.

If, in the same case, the court specifically orders Pat to pay child support even though the court has awarded Pat primary custody, it may be better to file a Motion to Reconsider – because now it is not certain whether the court made a mistake only regarding who was paying child support, or whether the court also made a mistake on who should have primary custody. If the court clarifies that it did intend to award primary custody to Pat and intended to order Jane to pay child support, Jane may want to file an appeal. Jane's basis for appeal might be that she believes the court should have awarded her primary physical custody of the children because she had been their primary caregiver during the marriage.

In a second example, the court awarded Eloise primary physical custody and child support, but the court did not award Eloise as much child support as she asked for. A *Nunc pro Tunc* would be appropriate if it appears the amount of the child support is in error. For example, Eloise asked for $1,220 per month, based on a calculation that was presented during trial. The court awarded Eloise $122 per month in child support. This could very well be a typo and the court may have meant to award Eloise the $1,220 she asked for.

On the other hand, if the court orders a completely different amount of child support, for instance $922, and it looks like there may have been an error in the calculation made by the court or an error in the numbers used for the calculation, a Motion to Reconsider may be the appropriate option. If the court orders $922 in child support and specifies that the reduction in the amount ordered is because the court is ordering the other parent to pay all out of pocket health care expenses, Eloise may want to appeal if she disagrees with the court. However, Eloise should consult with an attorney to consider how much the appeal will likely cost, compared to the amount of child support she might gain. The difference here is $298 per month or $3,576 per year, likely less than an appeal will cost. If the laws of her state allow her to request a child support adjustment in the future with much less cost than an appeal, an appeal may not be worth the cost on this issue.

Appeals

An Appeal asks a court that is higher than the trial court that heard your case, usually your state's court of appeals, to review the final order. The court of appeals cannot hear new evidence in your case. The court is limited to the record that was made during the trial.

The record includes transcripts of everything the court reporter recorded. This includes the testimony of the witnesses, the arguments made by the attorneys, and any rulings the judge made. The record also includes any exhibits that were offered and accepted by the court. The court of appeals will review the record and the order of the lower court and make a decision as to whether the final order is legally correct.

The court of appeals cannot make any separate assessment on whether the witnesses seem truthful, because they are not seeing the witnesses testify. For this reason, they will defer to the judgment of the trial court where such assessments of a witness's character are recorded. For example, if the trial court says that a key witness was untrustworthy because he squirmed in his seat every time he said good things about your parenting, the court of appeals will incorporate that assessment in its own view of the case.

Appeals can be expensive and time consuming. If the court of appeals does not decide the appeal in your favor, you can request that the state's supreme court review your case. Depending on your jurisdiction, there may be additional steps you must take before you can apply for your case to be considered by your state's supreme court.

Be aware that an appeal can open your case up for reconsideration on all issues. The other party will need to answer the appeal and may use this as an opportunity to appeal custody and child support too.

In Jane and Pat's case, since Pat will need to answer Jane's appeal, he might also counter appeal for additional child support. Pat can also ask the court to award him attorney fees and costs for having to answer the appeal. The cost of the appeal might outweigh the possible benefits, as in Eloise's case. Finally, the amount assessed by the court for things like alimony and child support could be based on the laws of your state and, therefore, an appeal will not help you. In Eloise's case, for instance, the laws in her state might have required that the judge reduce the child support by a specific amount if the parent paying the child support is required to cover all out-of-pocket health costs.

Your attorney should be able to advise you on whether an appeal is worth the added time and expense, as well as the likelihood that the court of appeals will rule in your favor. If your attorney does not do appellate work, he might need to refer you to an appeals attorney to evaluate your case and proceed with the appeal if necessary.

Post-Decree Requirements

Property settlements often require one or more assets to change ownership or be divided. For example, one party may need to sign over title in a motor vehicle or sign a quitclaim deed (a document that removes any claim one party might have over real property such as a house). You may also need to change ownership of debts by having a name removed from a credit card or by having a mortgage refinanced.

Some of these changes may have been made before the divorce was final, but those that have not been made will need to be dealt with soon after the decree is issued. The order might specify how many days the parties will have to make those changes.

Another common task will be to obtain a Qualified Domestic Relations Order (QDRO) to divide a retirement account. Some attorneys will do this for you. Others will facilitate having the QDRO done by a person or company that specializes in QDROs. A draft of the QDRO may need to be pre-approved by the administrator of the retirement plan (called the plan administrator) and then submitted to the court for a judge to sign. The signed order is then submitted to the plan administrator, and they will divide the retirement account as specified in the order.

You may also need a name change. If you have asked to have your premarital name restored, the court will grant that request in the final order. However, you will still need to use that order to officially have your name changed on all your documents and accounts.

Other agreements or orders may take some time. Assets may need to be sold and the proceeds divided, or one party may be required to pay the other party an amount of money in order to equalize the property distribution. This often happens when one party is awarded a substantial asset, like a home. The court or agreement may give the paying party several months or even several years to pay it off.

While you do not necessarily need to keep an attorney on retainer for this entire period of time, you may need to retain your previous attorney or a different attorney if there is a post decree issue.

For example, if the other party does not fulfill a post-decree requirement, you may have to ask the court to enforce the order. This request may be called an application for an Order to Show Cause, which asks the court to order the other party to come to court and show why they have not fulfilled the requirements in the decree. If the party does not have sufficient cause, the court can hold them in contempt, which could result in a fine, jail time, or other sanctions that the court finds just. The action is often called a contempt action. It can also apply to a party's failure to pay child support or alimony.

Modification

While an appeal is filed to correct a perceived defect in the original order, a Modification is filed to change an order because of a substantial change in circumstances. What changes qualify for a modification will vary by state and sometimes will vary by issue. For instance, the requirement to modify child support may be different than the requirement to modify custody. Property divisions may not be subject to modification except where alimony is considered a property division. Even then, alimony can be very difficult to modify.

You may not need to meet specific qualifications for the issue you want to modify if both parties agree to the modification. If the parties are not in agreement on a modification, the whole process can be as long and expensive as the initial divorce.

It is important to make reasonably sure that a divorce agreement is one you and your family can live with long term, because it can be a considerable expense to get it modified. You are not going to be able to anticipate everything that might happen after the divorce, but your attorney or other professionals in your team can talk to you about common issues that could cause modification. Some changes in circumstances, as in life, are going to be unavoidable.

Chapter 11

Basics of Court Etiquette

YOU WILL NOT GET A SECOND CHANCE to make a first impression on the court. Even the higher courts (your state's court of appeals and supreme court as well as the federal courts) rely on the first judge's opinion about the character of the witnesses and the parties during the trial. That means that the judge will put in the written order anything important about how you presented yourself in the courtroom.

For example, if your behavior in the courtroom gives the judge insight into whether you are being truthful, the judge will write about it in the final opinion, which will then be relied on by the higher courts if your case goes to appeal.

With that in mind, the following are some basics of court etiquette. Your attorney should go over any specific local court customs and best practices for conducting yourself in court. Sometimes your attorney will know certain things a local judge does not like. If your attorney does not offer to go over these things with you before a hearing or trial, ask them to do so.

For example, as a new attorney, I had a child welfare hearing in front of a judge in a rural county. I had never had an evidentiary hearing in front of this judge before. No one warned me about the judge's idiosyncrasies, and I was so new to the profession I did not think to ask. The first mistake I made was bringing a bottle of water into the courtroom, something which had been okay in all the other courtrooms I had previously been in.

The court attendant frantically waved for me to leave the courtroom, while pointing at my bottle of water. While she saved me from irritating the judge, I was instantly flustered.

Next, during my questioning of a social worker, I asked what concerns they had about the living conditions of the child. As soon as I said the word "concern," I could feel all eyes turn to me. What followed was the judge's angry rant about how we all have concerns, or he would not be hearing this case. Because I didn't know that the judge had an issue with the word "concern" in child welfare cases, I thought I had done something wrong, and it served to fluster me even further.

Of course, this is an extreme example. I have also heard stories of attorneys being asked to leave the courtroom because of their lack of etiquette or issues with how they are dressed. Judges are usually harder on attorneys who appear before them regularly, however, if your attorney tells you to do something or not to do something, it is coming from their experience with that judge.

As attorneys, we usually have access to specific rules for courtroom etiquette for each courtroom, county, or district. In some courtrooms, the attorneys are required to stand whenever they address the judge or a witness, while in other courtrooms, the attorneys are required to remain seated. Some states or courts have information about specific court etiquette for parties and sometimes for jurors.

While I am providing the most common etiquette standards and best practices, please ask your attorney for specific information. If you are representing yourself, look at the state or local judicial website.

In-Court Etiquette

You do not have to dress like your attorney does, wear clothing that represents your personal best. Do not wear dirty clothes, garments that have holes in them, or clothes with words or slogans on them. You do not want your clothes to make a statement to the court. You want to make sure the judge is listening to the evidence and testimony in your case, not to your clothes.

Do not chew gum in the courtroom. Do not bring food or drinks. Some courtrooms will allow you to bring in water, and some will supply water for the parties at counsel table.

Make sure your cell phone and any other electronics are silent or muted. If you have an electronic device that sometimes makes audible alerts and you do not know how to turn the alerts off, turn the device off completely or leave it at home.

Be aware of and in control of your body language. If you believe the other party, the other party's attorney, or a witness is being dishonest, it is your attorney's job to bring that to the attention of the judge. Refrain from rolling your eyes, sighing loudly, or otherwise signaling to the judge how you feel. Such body language is not communicating to the judge what you want it to communicate. Instead, the judge will see you as being dramatic, disruptive, disrespectful, and not in control of yourself. The impression you are giving the judge can be more important than whatever the witnesses are saying about you. If your behavior is repeatedly disruptive, the judge can exclude you from the courtroom, issue you a monetary sanction, or hold you in contempt. In an extreme case, the judge could send you to jail.

You want your body language to indicate to the judge that you are respectful of the judge, the courtroom and everyone in it, and the judicial process. You should sit still as much as possible, maintain your best posture, and do not make any unnecessary noise or comments. It is your attorney's job to present your side of the story to the judge. If you are worried about your attorney missing a key point or issue, write it down and discuss it with your attorney at a break. I always bring a spare notebook and pen for exactly this purpose.

If you do not have confidence in your attorney to present your case, you need to address those concerns before the trial.

If you have doubts about your attorney, first ask for a conference with your attorney to discuss your concerns. There may have been a miscommunication that can be resolved.

If you cannot resolve the issue, consider hiring a different attorney. While changing attorneys can be expensive, having an attorney who does not properly represent you can lead to an undesirable result that you will have to live with for many years to come, or that you will have to address in an expensive modification or appeal.

Do your best not to sidetrack or distract your attorney during a hearing or trial. Your attorney is on high alert. Not only do they need complete concentration when presenting an argument, asking questions of witnesses, or engaging with the judge or opposing counsel, your attorney also needs to pay attention to everything else being done and said in the courthouse (including being aware of your body language).

If you feel like you have something important to bring to your attorney's attention, write it down or wait until a break. Think of the hearing or trial like a well-scripted play. You would not interrupt a play to tell an actor they forgot a line; it is even worse for you to divert your attorney's attention at a critical moment. Your attorney knows best when they can multitask and will likely check in with you or look at your note pad when they can.

Virtual Hearing Etiquette

Virtual hearings have become common in many jurisdictions. Virtual hearings are often more flexible and can be a great solution to transportation issues and time. It can even save you money if your attorney charges for transportation time, mileage, and parking.

You might think of virtual hearings as being less formal, but you should treat them as though you are in the courtroom. While you might feel more comfortable because you are in a familiar setting, like your own home, there is more to consider than if you were in the courtroom. When you go in person, you only need to be concerned about your own appearance and etiquette. In a virtual hearing all the etiquette rules discussed above still apply, but you also need to make sure that everything the camera can see is appropriate. You will also need to think about noise levels and whether your internet connection will work adequately to get you through the hearing. You do not want your screen to freeze or to be disconnected during an important part of the hearing.

If you do not have a lot of experience with virtual meetings, or if you have not used the platform that the hearing will be held on, you may want to arrange a test run. Do your test run in the same place where you will be for the hearing. If you can, have a friend or family member log on to a meeting in the same platform the court will use. If that isn't possible, use any similar platform that is available. Your friend or family member can point out issues with sound or with your internet. You might think things are fine but for the other party, your screen might be freezing up, your microphone may not be working correctly, or there may be a background noise that you don't notice. These are things you may not be aware of from your side of the screen but that can be remedied before the hearing.

Discuss with your attorney how the two of you can communicate during the hearing if needed. Using the chat feature to communicate with your attorney during the hearing may not be confidential. The court may be able to read the chat comments, and if the hearing is recorded, a transcript of the chat may be saved with the hearing. Your attorney may want you to use your phone to text anything you need them to know, or the attorney may prefer you use a different online format.

You can also ask your attorney if you can join them at their office for the virtual hearing. Some attorneys may prefer that you be in the same room. If you are in the office with the attorney, you may be able to use the same method as you would in the courtroom, writing down the information or waiting until a break.

Telephone Hearing Etiquette

The two most important things in a telephone hearing are to make certain that you can hear what is going on and that the judge can hear you.

Try to avoid attending a telephone hearing with your mobile phone, because cellular phone reception can be unpredictable. If you must use your cell phone, find a place where you have reliably good reception and stay in one place. Do not drive around while attending a hearing with your cell phone. The judge will get irritated if the connection is bad and will be specifically irritated with you if they can tell that you are driving during the hearing. The judge is taking your case seriously, and they expect you to take your case seriously too.

If you cannot give the hearing your full attention on that day and time, ask your attorney if you can ask the court for a continuance (meaning to reschedule the hearing).

As in a virtual hearing, you will need to be aware of background noise. If you have chosen a specific place to be while you have your hearing, do a trial run by calling a friend or family member. They can tell you if they are hearing a lot of background noise or if the reception makes it hard to hear you. Consider using a headset if you have one, because it will cut down on background noise and may have a better microphone.

If there is some unavoidable background noise, you should mute your line whenever you do not need to be speaking. Make sure you pay attention to whether you are muted or not. I have had several telephone hearings where someone thought they were muted when they were not and accidently interrupted proceedings by talking to someone else in the house.

Chapter 12

OTHER PROFESSIONALS

YOUR ATTORNEY IS USUALLY NOT A COUNSELOR, coach, financial planner, business or real estate appraiser, parenting coordinator or tax professional. The good news is that you can hire any of those other professionals to be a part of your team. While you will have to pay each professional separately, it may cost you less than having your attorney do things they theoretically can do but are not specifically qualified to do. It may take your attorney twice as long, and their hourly rate is usually much more than any other professional on this list.

For instance, an attorney could, theoretically, do a market analysis on your home. This involves looking up homes in your neighborhood that have recently sold and are substantially similar to yours. Anyone with access to a computer can look up homes on a county assessor's page or on a website that specializes in listing or estimating property values. However, attempting to value your property in this way will take much longer for your attorney than for an experienced real estate agent, and the real estate agent is better qualified to determine what properties are really similar to yours. Real estate agents can also advise about whether the market has changed significantly since those homes sold.

Another example is asking your attorney about the merits of a particular settlement offer. Your attorney can easily advise on whether the settlement offer is better or worse than you are likely to get in trial. There are also going to be things that your attorney can readily see are not fair or equal. However, you should not ask your attorney to advise you on the tax consequences of that settlement, unless your attorney has some additional tax knowledge or qualifications.

Certified Divorce Financial Analyst

A Certified Divorce Financial Analyst (CDFA) can analyze the financial picture of your marriage and run scenarios for how to divide the assets and debts. Not only can the CDFA look at whether a particular settlement offer is fair, they can also show you how those assets will benefit (or not benefit) each party going forward given each party's budget, income, and potential tax consequences. A CDFA can be hired by either party, or by both parties as a neutral professional in a collaborative divorce. If hired by one party, a CDFA can testify in court for that party. A CDFA does not have to be an attorney or a financial professional; however, many CDFAs also work in either the financial or legal industry.

Suppose for example you want to keep the marital home and you are willing to give your spouse whatever other assets have accumulated in the marriage to make that happen. You understand it is going to be hard to afford the marital home on your own, but you think you can handle the financial details.

A CDFA would look at your budget, your income, and the tax consequences of the proposed settlement and might find that, five years from now, you will not be able to make your mortgage payment, or you will have to go into more debt to hold on to the house. This may be hard to hear, but it is better to know now than five years in the future when you are forced to sell the house.

This does not necessarily mean that you will have to give up the house, because a CDFA will be able to find a better solution if one is available. Suppose you believe it is best for you to keep the house because you want the children to continue living in their childhood home. Your spouse agrees that it is best for you to keep the house, yet they also want to pay the minimum of child support and alimony. You can hire a CDFA to show the other party how much support you are going to need in the coming years to keep the marital home. If the other party still does not agree and you are going to trial on that issue, the CDFA can testify in court for you.

I am also a Certified Divorce Financial Analyst (CDFA®), so I can give my clients some general advice about what to consider in the settlement. But, if my client needed a CDFA to run scenarios or testify in court, I would still advise them to get a separate CDFA. Hiring a CDFA will save them money (I charge half as much hourly when I am hired as a CDFA than when I am hired as an attorney). Additionally, if my client needed an expert to testify to the tax consequences of a particular settlement, I would not be able to testify as a CDFA while also serving as their attorney.

Other Financial Professionals

The other primary financial professionals you may want as part of your team are a certified public accountant (CPA) or a certified financial planner (CFP).

You and your spouse may have employed the services of a Certified Public Accountant (CPA) in the past. You may go to a CPA every year to prepare and file your taxes. If you are required to exchange or obtain tax returns, you can get them from your CPA. You may need to find a new CPA to help with your divorce if they have worked with both you and your spouse in the past.

If you are going through a collaborative divorce model or a mediation first model, you and your spouse may be able to consult the same CPA. A CPA can go over the returns with you if you are not familiar with them and help you understand the differences in taxable income and actual income for purposes of negotiating property settlement, child support, and spousal support. It might be hard to determine actual income without a CPA if one or both of you are self-employed.

A CPA can also value a business or analyze financial information in preparation for trial (also known as forensic accounting).

A Certified Financial Planner (CFP) can help you budget and plan for your financial future. You can meet with a CFP before the divorce is final to set up a financial plan for when your family is no longer in one household. The CFP can help you determine what you will actually need in property, retirement accounts, child support, and spousal support so that you will have a solid financial foundation after the divorce, and can testify in court if necessary.

While both CPAs and CFPs cost money, they can save you from costly mistakes in a divorce order or settlement.

Mediator

You may hear a Mediator referred to as a "third-party neutral," meaning that they do not represent either party and they do not have any investment in the outcome of your case. Having no interest in your case doesn't mean they don't care; it means that they will not have a personal gain or loss depending on the outcome of your case.

A Mediator is trained to help parties resolve any issues that they are having difficulty resolving on their own. This could be all aspects of your divorce or it could be one or more particular issues. You can hire a Mediator before either of you hire an attorney or start the court process, or you can hire a Mediator at any point in the divorce where you need help resolving an issue. Some states require you to attempt mediation before you can schedule a trial date. You can even go to a Mediator after the divorce to help you resolve disagreements without having to go to court again.

In most states, 40 hours of training is required to become a Mediator. A Mediator does not have to be an attorney. Since all Mediators have very similar training, you might want to choose your mediator based on what other experience they have. For instance, if the main issue in your divorce is custody, you may want a Mediator with custody experience such as an attorney, social worker, therapist, or custody evaluator.

Arbitrator

An Arbitrator is also a "third-party neutral," but, unlike a Mediator, an Arbitrator is hired to make decisions in your case. Each side will present their case to the Arbitrator, like presenting your case to a judge at trial, and the Arbitrator will make a decision on the issues you cannot agree on. That decision is usually binding, meaning a court will enforce it even if you want to back out of it later.

The benefit of going to an arbitrator instead of going to trial is that the parties can choose the Arbitrator, and you may be able to have your case heard much sooner than you would if you wait for a trial date. Depending on your state and local court, you could end up waiting a year or more for a trial date from the day that you file your petition.

Parenting Coordinator

A Parenting Coordinator is also a "third-party neutral" that can be hired to help both parents with co-parenting issues. A Parenting Coordinator is often used in high conflict cases where the parents are having great difficulty co-parenting.

Parenting Coordinators will make suggestions on how to handle parenting conflicts and will assist in developing or working within a parenting plan. They may also be called to testify at trial. A Parenting Coordinator is usually a mental health professional or an attorney.

Real Estate Agent

A real estate agent can be helpful in determining what your home or other real property is worth for purposes of settlement or sale. It is usually less expensive to pay a real estate agent to perform a market analysis on your property than it is to get an appraisal. Of course, a real estate agent can also help you sell your property either before or after the divorce is final.

Getting a real estate agent on your team early in the process will give you a better understanding of your net worth and, if you and your spouse are selling any real property, an idea of how long that process might take.

Expert Witness

An expert witness is different than any other witness because they have expertise in a particular area that is at issue in your case. There are many different expert witnesses who could be a part of your divorce. Most of the other professionals listed here can also be expert witnesses. Be aware that if you and your spouse have hired a professional jointly, that particular individual cannot be an expert witness for either one of you in the divorce. An expert witness might be called to testify about custody, property, disability, vocation, taxes, business valuation, or anything else that remains at issue in the divorce.

Therapist

Going through a divorce is not something we are innately equipped to handle. When you are in a pressure cooker of extreme stress, emotions can boil over. The stress of a divorce can also intensify mental health conditions that you may not even know you have. A therapist can help you navigate and get through this process. It is normal to have a lot of conflicting feelings: sorrow, grief, anger, and hurt, together with moments of happiness, excitement, and elation. Even if the emotions you are experiencing are what you consider to be mild, it can be helpful to have someone on your team who is qualified to help you through it.

Divorce Coach

You have probably heard about life coaches. A divorce coach is a life coach that specializes in helping people through the divorce process. The main difference between a life coach and a therapist is that a life coach helps you reach a particular goal or get through a particular issue or time in your life, while a therapist usually helps you with overall mental health issues. A life coach is not qualified to treat or diagnose mental health issues.

Life coaches are not well regulated. There are no requirements, certifications, or licenses on the state or federal level. There are private and nonprofit entities that certify life coaches, but the process and the training vary greatly.

For instance, I went through a 22-week certification program to become a life coach. As part of the certification process, I was required to coach other students while the rest of the class and instructor listened and gave feedback. I was also required to give 20 free sessions and pass a final exam. However, I also know a coach whose certification process took her only a weekend.

When choosing a divorce coach, consider the totality of life and professional experiences the coach has. For instance, while I did complete a life coach certification program, I am also a family law attorney with more than a decade of experience working with divorcing couples, and my undergraduate degree is in psychology.

You may want to hire a coach that has been through a divorce experience similar to yours, lives in your area, or hosts a support group. Many coaches offer a free get to know you session. If it is a good fit and the coach offers to work with you, don't be surprised if the coach wants you to buy more than one session up front. It takes time to begin to see results, and the coach may want you to commit to a certain number of sessions.

A divorce coach gives you someone to talk to about the parts of the divorce, like the emotional and personal impact, that your attorney is likely not qualified to help you with. A divorce coach usually costs less per hour than an attorney does, so hiring a divorce coach can save you money as well as give you better results.

You may decide that instead of talking to a professional, you will discuss those things with your friends and family. Hopefully, they will be able to support you. But while it may feel like they are helping you, in fact they may just be great at telling you what you want to hear. Also, friends and family will get worn out talking to you about your divorce, and your divorce may go on for a year or more.

Having someone who is paid to listen to you about your divorce and qualified to help you move towards goals and resolutions can help enormously. A divorce coach can also save you money by helping you work through things that are keeping you from reaching an agreement and, potentially, keep you from having to go to trial.

Vocational Consultant

If one party in the divorce has been staying home to take care of the children or the household and will now need to find a job, a vocational consultant can be helpful. A vocational consultant can help determine what job options are available and how much the job is likely to pay. The vocational consultant can also help determine how long it may take before the party seeking a job or career will be able to support themselves. In court a vocational consultant may be able to testify about how staying home has impacted a party's career and may be able to estimate the financial consequences of that impact.

A vocational consultant may also testify that a party is underemployed. This means that the underemployed party could be making more money at a job that better suits their education and experience; in other words, they could be better able to support themselves than it appears.

Here is an example of a situation where a vocation consultant would be of assistance. Eleanor went to school to be a teacher, but when she had kids, both she and her husband decided it would be more economically effective for Eleanor to stay home with the children and take care of the household. Eleanor worked in the home for twelve years and, now that she is getting divorced and her kids are older, she wants to go back to teaching.

A vocational consultant can help determine what it will take for Eleanor to update her teaching license and how long it will take her to get a teaching job. The vocational consultant can also testify about the impact that staying home for twelve years has had on Eleanor's teaching career. What would she be earning now if she had continued to be a teacher, instead of working in the home and taking care of the kids? What can she expect to earn when she does get a teaching job?

Chapter 13

SAFETY AND WELLNESS

THE NECESSARY ACTIONS TO TAKE CARE of your own safety and wellness are not automatically built into the legal divorce process. Your attorney may not initiate a discussion about your safety and wellness; however, both are very important to the process.

If you are not safe or do not feel safe, there are going to be additional considerations about how the divorce is handled. If you are not taking care of yourself, it can cause delays in reaching settlement or it may make the prospect of trial worse for you than it needs to be. The following are some considerations and tips for your safety and wellness.

DOMESTIC VIOLENCE

For a person in a domestically violent situation, the process of leaving the relationship can potentially be very dangerous. If there has been domestic violence in your marriage, it may change how your attorney or other professionals will advise you. Your attorney will need to know as soon as possible.

If the professionals on your team do not know about the domestic violence, they will not be able to advise you properly. As hard as it may be to tell them, it will be best for you if you do. If you are having a hard time telling your attorney, you may want to start with a therapist or divorce coach that can help you come up with a plan to approach the subject.

You and your attorney will need to work together to get your best possible outcome. While your attorney will be able to advise you of your options and will know the domestic violence laws in your state, you know your own situation best. You know more than your attorney does about how your spouse is likely to react to any potential course of action.

For example, some attorneys believe that mediation is never appropriate in divorce cases where there is domestic violence between parties. They argue that the objects of mediation cannot be realized if the participants in the mediation are not free to equally participate in the process because of fear or intimidation.

Yet, mediation may actually be helpful in deescalating the situation, if the mediation can be held safely. You can talk to your attorney about the typical mediation process in your location. Tell your attorney whether you believe that local mediation process will cause additional risks to your safety during or after the session. You can also discuss with your attorney anything that you believe will keep the mediation deescalated.

Mediators usually make sure that the parties are not in the same room together if there has been domestic violence. However, you may prefer to be in the same room so that your spouse knows everything you did or did not say, instead of imagining what you may have said in the other room.

If there is a no contact order between you and your spouse, then you will not be able to try mediation unless the order allows for it or modifications can be made to the order to allow it.

Some attorneys may also advise against a collaborative or cooperative model of divorce in the case of domestic violence, because they do not want you to be intimidated into a settlement that is not best for you. Yet, after being advised of your options you may still feel that a collaborative or cooperative model will keep the divorce less adversarial and therefore safer for you.

Again, you know your situation best. Your attorney can advise you about your best legal options, settlement options, and likely outcomes at trial, but you must make the decision that is best for you.

Attorneys are used to fighting for the best possible outcome for their clients, and that is usually measured in dollar amounts. You may have to remind your attorney about your non-monetary goals.

If there was domestic violence in your relationship, be aware that you may continue to have issues with your former spouse after the divorce. This can be especially true if you have children with your former spouse. An abusive person might use custody issues to continue a pattern of abuse. Even though you are divorced, if the abuse continues, it is still considered domestic violence in most states.

Recognizing Abuse

Abuse can be difficult to identify. I have had clients who are not sure if they are in an abusive relationship or not. I have had clients tell me that their spouse hits them, but they don't feel this is abusive because they hit back or because they believe they caused the abuse in some way. Emotional abuse is particularly hard to recognize.

Identifying whether there is abuse in your relationship will help you because, among other reasons, it may change you and your attorney's approach to the divorce process.

You may be surprised to learn that the actual definition of domestic violence does not center on physical violence alone. The National Domestic Violence Hotline defines Domestic Abuse as "a pattern of behaviors used by one partner to maintain power and control over another partner in an intimate relationship."

There are many forms of abuse and types of behaviors. Physical violence is just one. You may be experiencing several forms of abuse in one relationship. Domestic violence is usually about control.

If you think you may be in a domestically violent relationship, please seek more information. You can start at thehotline.org where you can browse resources, chat with someone online, text, or call them at 1-800-799-SAFE (7233). Also consider talking to a therapist, coach, doctor, friend, or your attorney.

Signs of Abusive Behavior (according to The National Domestic Violence Hotline website thehotline.org/resources/types-of-abuse).

1. Telling you that you never do anything right.
2. Showing extreme jealousy of your friends or time spent away from them.
3. Preventing or discouraging you from spending time with friends, family members, or peers.
4. Insulting, demeaning, or shaming you, especially in front of other people.
5. Preventing you from making your own decisions, including about working or attending school.
6. Controlling finances in the household without discussion, including taking your money or refusing to provide money for necessary expenses.
7. Pressuring you to have sex or perform sexual acts you're not comfortable with.
8. Pressuring you to use drugs or alcohol.
9. Intimidating you through threatening looks or actions.
10. Insulting your parenting or threatening to harm or take away your children or pets.
11. Intimidating you with weapons like guns, knives, bats, or mace.
12. Destroying your belongings or your home.

Wellness

There are events in our lives that are so monumental that we may not know how to process them. Divorce is one of those monumental events, even if you were the one who made the decision to divorce.

I highly recommend hiring a therapist or coach to help you navigate the emotional aspects of divorce. While support from your family and friends is great, divorce is a long process that, emotionally, begins well before the Petition is filed and continues long after the final decree has been signed. If you lean solely on your family and friends for your emotional wellbeing, and even if they wholeheartedly want to support you, you are going to wear them out. Unless they happen to have some education or experience in mental health, they will not be able to help you the way a professional can. Additionally, you can be free to talk to a professional about things that you may not be willing to tell your friends or family.

If you have children, they will be looking at how you are processing the divorce as an example of how they should be processing it. Taking steps to protect your own mental health will give you the strength to present a good example and help your children process the divorce. Additionally, a mental health professional can help you navigate what to tell your children and what you can do to help them. You may also want to give your children access to a mental health professional of their own. Some states have organizations specifically for helping children in divorce or in other court processes.

On the purely practical side, having a mental health professional on your team can save you time and money in your divorce. You will experience stress, sorrow, anger, and even grief in this process. When clients do not have someone to process these emotions with, the emotions tend to come out during decisive moments in the divorce process.

I have had cases that should have settled and indeed were about to settle when one of the unresolved emotions surfaced and prevented settlement. Those cases often end up with very similar results in the end, but between the failed agreement and the final agreement there are often many hours of unnecessary attorney fees and potentially an entire unnecessary trial. A therapist or coach could have prevented all that loss of time and money.

That Massage Can Save You Thousands

Wellness might seem like just another self-help buzzword, but when going through divorce, taking appropriate care of yourself can save you time and money. How you are taking care of yourself, or not taking care of yourself, will influence your ability to think clearly and make decisions that will impact your life for years to come.

A weekly massage, for example, can be well worth the cost if it helps you reduce stress, anxiety, or anything else that is holding you back, and thus help you to navigate the divorce process with your own best interests in mind. It can, ultimately, save you thousands in attorney fees. That massage can help you retain information better, and you will be less likely to ask your attorney to repeat answers you have already been given. You will be able to make better decisions and make them more quickly. You are less likely to make an agreement that will have a negative impact on your life going forward. You may be able to avoid having to modify an order in the future.

Of course, massage is not the only way to nurture yourself. There are many wellness strategies that can give you the same benefits. The following are ten strategies that are easy, free, and do not take a lot of time.

Ten Strategies to Promote Wellness

Be Mindful

You don't have to meditate for an hour a day or go on a meditation retreat. You don't have to follow a guru or read a bunch of books. You can spend just minutes a day practicing mindfulness and get big results.

As soon as you read the word "meditate," you probably conjured an image of a person sitting cross-legged, arms slightly out from their body, pointer finger and thumb making a circle on both hands. However, there are many different ways to meditate or practice mindfulness. You can get free guided meditations online, you can do a walking meditation, or you can just have a moment of quietness where you practice clearing your mind.

The emphasis is on "practice." Clearing your mind is something you practice doing. You are not expected to master it, nor do you have to master it in order to achieve results. The point is not to control your thoughts, but to engage in practicing control over your thoughts. Not only will this have overall effects on your state of mind, but it can also help you during moments of feeling acutely stressed and overwhelmed, as you become able to practice mindfulness in the moment.

Breathe

Breathing exercises are like mindfulness in that they pull your focus from what is stressful or upsetting and put it on your breathing instead. In meditation, you are practicing control over your thoughts by ignoring them or clearing them from your mind, during breathing exercises you are practicing control by refocusing your thoughts. There are many different types of breathing exercises, and you can find guides online.

Eat

If you are not getting proper nutrition, your ability to do anything else is compromised. This is not the time to start a restrictive diet, nor is it a time to indulge in food that makes you feel unhealthy and clouds your mind. This is the time to feed yourself like you would feed your child. Make sure you are getting enough to eat, and that the quality of your food is the best that you can provide for yourself.

Move

Exercise does not have to be grueling or time consuming to be effective. You should not be training for the Olympics during your divorce. Simple movement can have a long-term positive impact, but it can also help you through times of extreme stress. Even getting up and stretching or pacing can help calm and focus you. This is a strategy you can use during high stress situations during your divorce. You can ask for a break or excuse yourself to use the restroom during meetings or mediations. You can pace while talking to your attorney on the phone. You can take advantage of breaks during trial by getting up and walking around or stretching out in the hall. Simply raising your arms above your head in a stretch can relieve stress and boost your confidence.

Be Social

Studies have shown that interacting with others can help improve stress and mood. This can happen even while engaging in small talk with strangers. For a bigger wellness boost, make a point to spend positive time with friends and family. You can also be social while engaging in movement by inviting a friend or family member to walk with you or by joining an exercise class.

Sleep

Getting enough sleep is vital to your wellbeing. However, it can be difficult to achieve a good night's sleep when you are stressed out. Using some of the other methods on this list can also help you sleep. While you can't make yourself sleep, you can make sleep a priority. Make sure your schedule allows for you to have uninterrupted sleep time when possible. If you are struggling with sleep, consider talking to your doctor.

Visualize

Using visualization is another form of refocusing your attention. You can do it anytime and anywhere. You can think of a happy place and visualize being there. I like to visualize being on a beach and imagine I can hear the waves. This visualization is especially helpful to me when I am having difficulty falling asleep.

You can also visualize the future. Even if you do not want to be divorced, visualizing your future after the divorce can still be positive, because you can visualize a more peaceful future where you are no longer going through the divorce process. Visualizing future events can also help give you a sense of control.

Smell the Roses

In the literal sense, interacting with nature can reduce your stress. If you are not likely to be able to go outside often, you can bring nature to your indoor spaces by adding plants or even paintings or pictures of nature.

In the metaphorical sense, taking time for the little things in life can also help refocus your attention and reduce your stress. You can combine this strategy with other techniques on this list. For example, you can take time to be social on a small scale by engaging in friendly banter with a coworker or even with your barista on the way to work.

Laugh

As they say, laughter is the best medicine. Laughter can reduce stress and refocus your mind. You can combine this strategy with several others. You can have a laugh with someone else while being social. You can entertain yourself with a comedy show or movie. There are even forms of laughter meditation. You can find laughter meditation guides online.

Escape

Have you ever watched a movie or television show that is so good you forgot all your problems for that short time? You can take a mini vacation from your worries by entertaining your brain with movies, books, music, plays, and art.

Chapter 14

FREQUENTLY ASKED QUESTIONS

THIS SECTION INCLUDES THE QUESTIONS I am most often asked. The answers will always depend on your state and local laws and on your specific situation. My aim is to give you a general overview of the topic and the various considerations that will influence the answer in your specific case.

How much will this cost?

The cost of your divorce will depend on several things. Your location greatly influences the cost. The hourly rate attorneys in your area charge will be relative to the cost of living in the area. For instance, a divorce in California, like the overall cost of living, will cost more than a divorce in Iowa.

Other differences in your state laws might influence the amount of work and time needed for a divorce, which will also influence the cost. Within your state and local jurisdiction, the next biggest factor is whether the divorce is contested. You can save money if you and your spouse have already decided on the terms of your divorce and only need an attorney to draft documents. However, you can lose more money than you save if you settle for something that is not equitable just because you want to save money on attorney fees.

If you and your spouse have minor children together, the divorce will cost more both in time and money.

The attorneys chosen by you and your spouse will obviously be a factor in the total cost, not only because of their hourly fees but because of their style of practice. One attorney may increase the cost significantly by filing unnecessary pleadings or by not responding to the other attorney in a timely way.

Conversely, how you and the other party proceed as clients will also influence the bottom line. If either party contacts their attorney several times a week, obviously the divorce costs will go up for both parties. Or, if either party is unresponsive, causing the attorneys to reach out multiple times for each issue, the bill will go up.

The type of divorce you choose will also influence the cost, but it can also help keep other factors in check by regulating the type and frequency of communication going back and forth between the attorneys. For instance, if you are in a collaborative divorce with regularly scheduled meetings, the parties and attorneys are less likely to reach out in between meetings because they know they can bring up issues during the meeting.

How long will it take?

Some states specify certain timelines including how long the divorce must be pending before a final order can be filed. For instance, in Iowa, there is a 90-day waiting period between when the divorce is served on the Respondent and when the final decree can be entered. In some circumstances the waiting period can be waived.

Beyond the timelines required by the court, the biggest influence on time is how many contested issues there are in your divorce and whether you will need to go to trial. The same factors at play in the cost also influence the time and for the same reasons.

Do I need an attorney?

The short answer is yes. To the extent that you can afford to hire an attorney, you should do so, even if that means you can only hire an attorney for an hour to go over your specific situation with you. For the cost of one attorney hour, you could potentially save yourself thousands of dollars and hours of time. It always costs more in both time and money to correct mistakes than to pay an attorney to help you avoid those mistakes.

I know that not everyone can afford an attorney or afford full representation. That is part of the reason why I wrote this book. The knowledge you can gain here is going to save you hours of attorney fees. However, it is well worth it to hire an attorney for as much assistance as you can afford.

What if I can't afford an attorney?

Check in your local area for free, reduced, or sliding scale legal services. You can start with the local bar associations. These are organizations of attorneys who practice in a particular location. There may be a county bar association and a state bar association where you live. Some bar associations have projects or clinics where lawyers volunteer their services to assist clients who can't afford to pay. These are often called Volunteer Lawyers Projects. Even if they can't help you directly, the local bar association should know what resources are available in your area.

I do not recommend calling attorneys and asking them to represent you for free. As professionals, it is expected of us to do a certain amount of volunteer or *pro bono* work (*pro bono* means for the good). However, many attorneys do that work through state or county run volunteer lawyers projects, where the intake assessment of clients has already been done and there may be access to funds to cover expenses and filing fees.

Other attorneys prefer to do their *pro bono* work in legal clinics that might be run by a school or other agency for a specific legal purpose. Other attorneys may prefer to do their *pro bono* work in areas of law they do not usually practice in. If you set up a consultation just to ask for free services, you are wasting the attorney's time and your own.

Can't I represent myself?

You can represent yourself partially or fully. Representing yourself is usually referred to as being "*pro se.*" This book is a good place to start to give you an overview of what you will be taking on. Read chapter 6 on the divorce process. Also refer to chapter 4 for more information about representing yourself.

If I move out before the divorce, will I forfeit my property rights in the marital home?

You will not give up any legal property rights to the marital home by moving out.

However, be aware that judges, like rivers, will often take the path of least resistance. If you both want to keep the marital home, but you have not been living in it during the divorce process, the judge may order that your spouse keep the marital home. That being said, in some circumstances it may be well worth moving out, even if that means you will not get to keep the marital home, especially if you feel unsafe or there is constant fighting.

If you do not get to keep the home, you will still get an equal or equitable share of the marital property depending on your state's law. You may receive your half of the value in the home by keeping a different asset, or your spouse may have to make payments to you to equalize the property division. If you live in an equal property distribution state, the judge will try to split the marital property so that each person gets as close to fifty percent as possible. If you live in an equitable property division state, the judge will try to split the marital property so that each person's share is as fair as possible. Often an equitable distribution is close to a fifty-fifty split, but it gives the judge more discretion to change the division based on the situations of the parties.

I have also been asked about the saying that "possession is nine-tenths of the law." The short answer it that the saying is an expression, it is not actual law.

Clients have told me that they have received the opposite advice from other attorneys, friends who have gone through divorce, or through information they saw online. Out of curiosity I have searched the internet and have found articles telling people not to move out of the marital home. I have even seen "moving out before the divorce is final" listed as one of the top mistakes you can make. The reasons given vary but seem to be, in general, the idea that the judge will see your decision to move out as a decision to abandon the marriage, the home, and the children. This may be a concern in states that still require fault in divorce if one of the grounds is abandonment. However, when fault is not an issue, I think this advice is dangerous as a blanket rule, because it can make an already tense or even dangerous situation worse if both parties are refusing to leave.

Isn't my retirement account my own property?

Any money earned during the marriage is marital property. It is helpful in this sense to think of your marriage as a business partnership.

For example, Sally and Steve have a partnership selling seashells. Sally goes out to the beach every day and gathers seashells. Steve stays at the seashell store and sells the seashells. Sally is worried about what will happen if she is ever unable to physically gather seashells, so Sally and Steve decide that every time Sally goes to the beach to collect seashells, she will put some of them aside. In that way, on days when she is sick or otherwise unable to go to the beach, they will still have seashells to sell. At some point Sally and Steve decide they no longer want to be in business together and they decide to dissolve the partnership. They take all the property (or assets) of the business and the debts of the business and divide them evenly. It makes sense that the seashells that have been saved are property of the business and are not the sole property of Sally just because she is the one that saved them. The seashells should either be sold, and the proceeds divided, or the seashells should be split evenly between them.

If you substitute wages for the seashells and marriage for the business, you have the same scenario with the wages you have set aside in a retirement account for when you are no longer able to work. These wages are still the property of the marriage if they were earned during the marriage.

If some of the funds were earned before the marriage, there are formulas to determine what the marital share is. Keep in mind, if you only worked a short time outside the marriage, it may cost more to determine what the marital share is than it is worth, in that case you may still want to split it in half. Sometimes both parties have a retirement account, and it is less expensive for each party to keep their own account than to split each account. Or you may decide to deduct an amount from just one of the retirement accounts to even them out.

It is also common for one party to trade the value they are entitled to in a retirement account in exchange for keeping the value of the equity in the marital home or some other asset. If you have a friend who tells you they got to keep their entire retirement account, there might be more to the story than they are telling you. They may not even understand how the property distribution worked. You cannot rely on how someone else's divorce went. Divorces are all very specific to individual circumstances and jurisdiction.

What about my inheritance or gifts from my family? Are those marital property?

In most states inheritance or gifts are not marital property. However, be aware that an inheritance or gift can become marital property, depending on how you use it.

For instance, suppose you receive an inheritance or gift of $10,000 from a family member. You take that money and deposit it in a joint marital account. You don't use it on anything specific, but it becomes a cushion for unexpected expenses over the years. It may be impossible to determine where that money went, and a court might find that it is inequitable to require the marriage to pay that money back to you as an individual.

On the other hand, suppose you inherit a vacation cabin and $10,000. You might keep the cabin in your name only and pay all repairs, taxes, or mortgages from a separate account where the only money deposited was your inheritance money. In the divorce, that property might be determined to be your sole and separate property.

However, most cases are not that clear. More often, even if the property is kept as separate property, the expenses might be paid with marital property. In that case, the appreciation in value of the property may be viewed as marital property. In the same example above, suppose you inherited the vacation cabin and no money. You still kept the cabin in your name only, but you paid expenses and taxes out of martial funds. The cabin was worth $50,000 when you inherited it and now it is worth $100,000. A judge may decide that $50,000 of it is your separate inherited property but that the other $50,000 is marital property.

Is there an advantage to filing first?

There is no huge legal advantage to filing first. By filing first, you may be able to choose the venue if there is more than one appropriate venue (location) to file the divorce in. However, if you both live in the same county, there will likely be only one venue where the divorce can be filed.

Depending on the law or local rules where you file, the person who files might have some choices in who presents evidence first in a trial or may have some additional control over the proceedings. A local attorney will know of any particular advantages that Petitioners have in your local area, if any.

The person who files first will have, at least initially, slightly more attorney fees because it takes more time to draft and file the Petition than it will take to answer the petition. The Petitioner will also have to pay filing fees. Those fees can be split later by agreement or by order of the court, or the Petitioner may just be stuck with that cost.

There may be a perceived advantage because the Petitioner can request a default if the other party does not answer, but that will only happen if the Respondent does not answer or if the Petitioner fraudulently claims that the Respondent was served when they were not served. In either case there is no real advantage, because default orders can be set aside.

One personal advantage you may have if you file first is a sense of control over the divorce. By choosing when the divorce is filed you will be able to prepare yourself and will not be taken by surprise. This can be especially helpful if you know that once the divorce is filed the other party might become uncooperative at best or hostile at worst. You can prepare yourself by putting together the documents and resources that you need in advance. You may also need to line up alternative housing so that you will not have to live with an angry or hostile spouse while the divorce is pending.

Can I get Alimony?

The factors that determine whether spousal support (alimony) is appropriate vary in each state. Usually, the considerations include the length of the marriage and the ability of each party to earn an income that will support the standard of living they enjoyed during the marriage.

Spousal support is calculated differently depending on the state, and some states do not have a clear formula for calculation. Spousal support can be awarded for different lengths of time. If it is anticipated that the spouse receiving support will eventually be able to support themselves, the spousal support may only be awarded for the period of time it will take for that person to start making an adequate income. Other spousal support awards may be for the life of the spouse being supported or until the spouse who is paying retires.

Sometimes spousal support awards are property settlements in disguise. Some states allow spousal support to be reconsidered if the spouse being supported remarries, begins to cohabitate with a significant other, or becomes engaged.

What's Next?

THROUGH THE KNOWLEDGE IMPARTED in this book, you can move forward in your divorce, empowered to make the choices that will work best for you. You have a resource that will save you time and money and will serve as a map through the divorce process. I hope that this book will help reduce feelings of helplessness. Divorce is difficult, so be nice to yourself and know that it will get better.

If you are going through a divorce or contemplating divorce, know that you are not alone. If you need additional help or resources, please go to http://www.greenberglawia.com. Also, look for more books in this series at http://www.wheretostartbooks.com. Look for upcoming titles on children in divorce and financial aspects of divorce. Join us on Facebook at Greenberg Law or Where to Start Books. Lastly, consider joining my divorce support group on Facebook at Where to Start: Divorce Support.

Glossary of Terms

MANY WORDS USED IN THE DIVORCE PROCESS have very specific legal meanings which differ from their ordinary use. This list of terms will help you understand the meaning of these words as they relate to divorce specifically.

50/50 Custody

See shared care.

Acceptance of Service

The Petitioner must prove to the court that the Respondent has received the Petition, the Civil Original Notice, and any other documents required by the court. The Petitioner can give the documents to the Respondent and ask the Respondent to sign a document stating that the documents were received. The document the Respondent signs is called an Acceptance of Service and must be filed with the court. If the Respondent will not sign the document, the Petition must be given to the Respondent through Process Service. See Process Service.

Admissions

Part of the discovery process, where a series of statements are sent to the opposing party. The opposing party can either admit or deny each statement.

In some courts, a failure to respond to the statements within the required time can mean that they are all deemed admitted.

Affidavit

A written and sworn statement that is signed by the party making the statement. An affidavit is used instead of testimony when allowed. It usually needs to be notarized.

Alimony

See Spousal Support.

Alternative Dispute Resolution

There are several types of Alternative Dispute Resolution (ADR). The purpose of all of them is to avoid going to trial. Mediation and Arbitration are the more well-known types of ADR. Mediation is the form of ADR you are most likely to encounter during your divorce, because many courts now require Mediation before you can get a trial date. If you are not able to resolve all the issues in your divorce, ADR is an alternative to having your dispute settled by trial. Instead, you can choose to hire a neutral person who does not have any investment in the outcome of your case and is trained to help others resolve disputes.

Alternative Service

The Petitioner must prove to the court that the Respondent has received the Petition and any other documents required by the court. If the Petitioner is unable to prove that the Respondent has received these documents through an Acceptance of Service or through Process Service, the Petitioner can apply to the court for Alternative Service. Typically, Alternative Service is by publication, meaning a notice is published in a newspaper.

Annulment

Annulment means that the entire marriage is set aside or made void because one of the parties proves there was fraud in obtaining the marriage or there is a defect in the marriage itself. For instance, a marriage may be annulled because it is discovered that one of the parties to the marriage was already married. Some states will allow an annulment if the marriage has not yet been consummated.

Answer

The Respondent, after being served, will have a set amount of time to Answer the Petition. The Answer is a document that responds directly to the Petition by declaring which paragraphs the Respondent agrees or disagrees with (usually written as "admit" or "deny").

Appeal

If the court enters a ruling that one of the parties disagrees with, that party can ask a higher court, usually the Court of Appeals, to review the ruling. The party appealing will write an appeal brief and the other party will have an opportunity to respond. An appeal can be time-consuming and expensive.

Appearance

An attorney can declare that they are representing a party in a case by filing a document called an Appearance. The Appearance states who the attorney will be representing and the attorney's contact information. The Appearance may also specify what representation will or will not include (often called a Limited Appearance). In some courts an attorney can "appear" by filing a pleading—for instance, if the attorney files the Petition in the case. Parties to the case may also "appear" by filing a pleading, filing a response to a pleading, through their attorney's filed Appearance, or by attending a hearing in court either in person or through an attorney.

Arbitration

A form of Alternative Dispute Resolution where the parties agree to settle a matter outside of court. An arbitrator is not a judge (but may be a retired judge). An arbitrator is hired to hear the case and decide on the outstanding issues in the case. Most contracts, from a mortgage to a gym membership, will have what is called an Arbitration Clause. By signing the contract, you agree that any disputes that arise out of the contract will be settled in Arbitration. Depending on the agreement you make, the arbitrator's decision may or may not be final.

Child and Family Reporter (CFR)

In Iowa, a Child and Family Reporter (CFR) may be appointed to a case where minor children are involved. They may be appointed because the court decides that a CFR would be beneficial or because one or both parents has requested one. The role of the CFR is to investigate the case, mostly through interviewing the parties, the children, and any person the CFR believes has important information. The CFR then writes a report about what they found and files it with the court. The purpose of the report is to provide the judge with information that should be unbiased. A CFR, unlike a *Guardian Ad Litem*, does not represent any of the parties in the case and should be neutral. A CFR might be an attorney or a person of another profession, for example, a social worker. Other states may have a CFR equivalent under a different title.

Child Support

An amount of money paid by a parent (the payor) to a party who is physically caring for the children (the payee). The payee is usually the other parent. However, in some cases the payee is a relative or guardian who is taking primary care of the child.

Child support is often determined by looking at the combined income of the family and determining how much of that total income would be allocated to financially supporting the child. The amount each person will pay toward the maintenance of the child is based on the percentage of the family's income they bring in. For instance, if parent one makes $50,000 and parent two makes $150,000, then parent one will be responsible for twenty-five percent of the support amount, and parent two will be responsible for seventy-five percent of the support. If parent two has primary physical custody, then it is assumed that parent is providing their portion of the support directly to the children. In this scenario, parent one will then pay their twenty-five percent to parent two.

In the case of shared custody or 50/50 custody, the support is calculated as if one parent has primary physical custody and then recalculated as if the other parent has primary physical custody. The two amounts are compared and then offset to determine if either parent will pay the other support. For instance, suppose parent one would have been required to pay parent two $400 a month for child support if parent two had primary physical care, and parent two would have been required to pay parent one $600 a month if parent one had primary physical care. If the parties have shared custody, in this scenario, parent two would still pay parent one $200 a month.

The assessed amount of child support may seem like too much to the payor and may seem like too little to the payee. This is because the family still has the same amount of income but now those funds are supporting two different households. Depending on your state and the particular judge assigned to your case, you may be able to agree on an amount that is different than the court would assess, if there is a good reason to do so.

Collaborative Divorce

Collaborative is a model of divorce where the parties agree that they will collaborate in designing a divorce settlement. This settlement is designed through a series of several meetings of the parties with their attorneys and other professionals. Collaborative law requires the parties to sign an agreement that they will not go to trial. If they later wish to go to trial instead, they will have to get new attorneys. For more details, see Chapter 2: Divorce Models.

Conciliation

Your state may require a period of time for the parties to engage in conciliation services before a divorce can be granted. This could include marital counseling, mediation, or other services aimed at resolving the party's differences so that they can remain married.

Conflict of Interest

You may hear from a potential attorney or another professional that they cannot take your case or work on your case because they have a conflict of interest. A conflict of interest means that the attorney or other professional is currently or has previously worked on a case or with a person who may have concerns that are not compatible with yours.

For example, when you call a prospective attorney, they will have some method for searching for your name and the name of your spouse in their records in order to determine if they have represented either of you before. Suppose they find they represented your spouse a few years ago in a real estate transaction. This may seem unrelated, but in doing so they may have learned all about your spouse's assets and debts, credit, and employment. These things may be useful to know in representing you, but they still owe a duty of confidentiality to your spouse. It would be a conflict to now represent you because the attorney cannot disclose anything they know from having worked for your spouse, even if it can help you.

This is only one scenario. There are many other situations that could constitute a conflict of interest. They may not be able to tell you what the conflict of interest is without revealing information they cannot ethically reveal, they may only be able to tell you that they cannot work with you.

In some very narrow exceptions, there may be a situation that appears to be a conflict of interest but is not a true conflict of interest. In that case the attorney or other professional may have you or another party sign a document stating that the attorney or other professional has explained the potential conflict of interest, but that the party wants to move forward with that professional anyway. For an attorney, this should only happen if the attorney finds that there is no likelihood that representation will actually cause a conflict.

Contempt

If a party does not comply with a court order, that party may be found in contempt of court. The contempt may occur in front of the judge, but more often, it occurs outside of court and is a violation of a written ruling. To bring a contempt to the attention of the court, a party may file an Application for Order to Show Cause. This pleading may have a different name in your state.

An example of an in-court contempt would be if a party is told to remain quiet and continues to talk. In that case, the judge can find that party in contempt directly.

An example of an out of court contempt would be if a party is ordered to pay child support and fails to do so. In this case, the contempt would have to be brought to the attention of the court. The court will then issue an order to show cause, stating that the party accused of contempt will have to appear in court and show why they should not be found in contempt. If the party is found in contempt or agrees that they are in contempt, the court has several options on what sanctions to issue, including monetary fines and jail time. A party in contempt may also be given the opportunity to cure that contempt. For example, if a party is found in contempt for failing to pay child support, the court may give that party an opportunity to pay all the child support that is owed. The court may then require the party to continue to pay child support on schedule for a period of time before the contempt case will be dismissed.

Contested

If there are any issues that the parties do not agree on, then the divorce is contested. This does not necessarily mean that the divorce is or will be combative. However, if the case is contested, an attorney will factor that into the retainer or flat fee, because it means there will be more work to do to resolve the issues through negotiation, mediation, or trial.

Continuance

A continuance is a fancy way of saying that a hearing will be rescheduled, or sometimes a deadline is reset. Either party can request a continuance, and the court can also order a continuance on its own. Continuances can be frustrating to parties who are expecting an issue to be resolved by a certain time.

Custody

Custody is a term to describe who is caring for children. There are two kinds of custody—physical custody and legal custody.

Physical custody describes the arrangement for the children's physical care. If you have primary physical custody, that means the children live with you most of the time and visit or have parenting time with the other parent. If you have shared physical custody (also called shared care or 50/50 custody), the children are physically cared for equally by the parents.

Legal custody describes the legal care arrangement. If you have joint legal custody (or 50/50 legal custody), which is usually the default arrangement, the parents equally share in the decision-making process for the children on things like school, extracurricular activities, medical decisions, and religion. If you have sole legal custody, you are the sole decision maker. Sole legal custody is rare and usually happens when one parent has done something to demonstrate that they cannot or should not be making decisions for the children, or because the parents cannot get along well enough to make decisions together.

Default

If the Respondent does not answer the Petition, the Petitioner can start the default process. Each state will have specific rules on how to obtain a default in divorce proceedings.

In Iowa, the Petitioner must first mail a notice of default to the Respondent. If there is no response in ten days, the Petitioner can then ask the court to set a default hearing. If the Respondent does not respond and does not appear at the hearing, the judge may enter a default order.

While it might seem like this is an excellent way to get what you want in a divorce, the default order can be contested. If the Respondent later appears and has a good reason why they did not appear, especially if it was because the Petitioner failed to serve the Respondent properly, the order can be set aside, and proceedings will start again at the answer stage.

It is worth making every effort, even beyond the efforts required by the court, to notify the Respondent so that a final divorce order—rather than a default—can be achieved. However, if the Respondent will not cooperate or cannot be found, a default prevents a case from continuing indefinitely.

Depositions

Depositions are a process by which a witness can be interviewed with a court reporter present but outside the presence of the judge. Depositions may be scheduled as part of the discovery process. Sometimes Depositions are taken because a witness will not be able to testify in court.

Because Depositions can show what the parties and witnesses will testify to in a trial, it can help parties prepare for trial or even help to settle the case.

Transcripts of the Depositions are usually not admissible in the trial if the witness is available to testify live during the trial. However, if a party testifies differently in trial than they did in the Depositions, the transcripts can be used to impeach the witness, meaning that they will be used to show that the witness lied during the Deposition or is lying in court.

Discovery

Both parties can use the discovery process to learn facts about the case in preparation for a trial. Discovery can include depositions, requests for production of documents, interrogatories, and admissions. State laws usually set limits to what can be requested in the discovery process.

Discrete Legal Services

See Unbundled Services.

Disposition

The Disposition is the outcome of the case. In a divorce the Disposition will likely be an order or decree from the court stating that the parties are no longer married and setting out the terms of the divorce.

Dissolution

Divorce can also be called a Dissolution or a Dissolution of Marriage.

Fault

In the past, a party had to demonstrate fault to be granted a divorce, meaning the party seeking the divorce would have to prove that the other party did something to destroy the marriage. Some examples of alleged fault were infidelity, inability to have sexual intercourse, abandonment, cruelty, and insanity. Some states still require a demonstration of fault; however, most states are "no-fault" states.

Flat Fee

Some attorneys will offer a flat fee divorce as an alternative to an hourly rate. The benefit to a flat fee is knowing exactly what your divorce will cost and not having to worry about paying extra for things like calling your attorney. If your attorney offers a flat fee, make sure you understand what is included and what is not included. A flat fee arrangement typically will not include a trial. The cost of the trial may be determined separately, if a trial is needed.

Guardian ad Litem (GAL)

Guardian ad Litem literally translates into guardian for the legal action. A *Guardian ad Litem* is like an attorney (and in some states is an attorney) who represents the best interests of a party. A *Guardian ad Litem* is assigned when a party is legally unable to speak for themselves, such as a minor child or an incarcerated party.

Hearing

Hearings may be set for several different reasons during your divorce. A hearing is different from a trial in that it often deals with one issue or a small number of issues. The decision in a hearing is often temporary or may involve issues of procedure. The court may limit the kind of evidence that is presented. Some courts will only allow written affidavits and arguments for a hearing.

A common example is a hearing on temporary matters, held to determine things like custody and support on a temporary basis until the matter can be heard at trial. An example of a procedural hearing would be if one party is disputing a procedural matter, such as whether the matter has been filed in the right jurisdiction. Hearings are usually much shorter than trials, possibly as short as thirty minutes.

Interrogatories

Interrogatories are a written list of questions that the parties may send to each other during discovery. The party receiving the list of questions usually has a set number of days to answer the questions in written form. The answer may be a legal objection to the question.

If you are served with interrogatories, your attorney will go over what questions you should answer and what questions can be objected to or partially objected to. If a party does not respond or if the party responds with objections to the questions, the other party can file a Motion to Compel, asking the court to compel the party to answer the questions. The court will likely set a hearing to determine whether the answers should be compelled or whether there is a legitimate reason why the party has not answered the interrogatories.

Legal Custody

See Custody.

Limited Appearance

Some courts will allow an attorney to make a limited appearance in a case to provide limited or specified services on behalf of a client. After the attorney has fulfilled the object of the limited appearance, the attorney can end the appearance and will no longer be representing the client. In contrast, when an attorney makes a general appearance, that attorney is expected to represent the client throughout the entire case unless they withdraw or apply to withdraw their appearance.

Mediation

Mediation is a form of **alternative dispute resolution** (ADR), meaning that it is an alternative to going to trial. Mediators are trained to help parties resolve their issues. Mediators do not make decisions in your case but rather assist you and your spouse to reach an agreement on your own terms.

Motion

There may be various motions filed in your case. Motions are generally used to request something of the court, such as setting a date for a hearing, requesting more time to comply with an order, or enforcing an order.

No Contact Order

Also known as a restraining order. A No Contact Order (NCO) orders one individual, known as the Defendant or Respondent, to stop having any contact with another individual, known as the Plaintiff or Protected Party. NCOs can be entered as part of a criminal case, for instance in a domestic abuse or assault case. An NCO can also be requested by an individual in civil court.

An NCO will be specific to your situation, so it may allow contact for a narrow scope of communication. For instance, if the Plaintiff and the Respondent have children together, the NCO might allow written contact regarding the children only.

Depending on your state, an NCO may offer other relief for domestic violence, such as temporary possession of a home and temporary custody of children.

Nunc Pro Tunc

Latin term that translates to "now for then." A Motion for a *Nunc Pro Tunc* is appropriate where there are errors in an order. A new order is issued that supersedes the previous order or part of an order. For more information, see chapter 10, The Divorce Process: After the Divorce.

Order to Preserve Assets

Either party can ask the court for an Order to Preserve Assets by filing a Motion to Preserve Assets. This order will restrict what the parties can do with the assets of the marriage while the divorce is pending. It can order that neither party sell anything (like a car, real estate, etc.). It can also restrict what money can be spent, usually only money for ordinary expenses. This can help prevent a party from wasting assets or attempting to keep them from the other party.

Paralegal

Paralegals are trained to conduct legal research and writing, prepare legal forms, and other tasks that do not require direct representation of a client. Paralegals require the supervision of an attorney. Your attorney may have a paralegal who assists with cases and may bill a lower hourly fee for the time the paralegal spends on your case.

Paraprofessional

A very small number of states have a designation somewhere in between a paralegal and an attorney called a paraprofessional, a legal paraprofessional, or paralegal practitioner. A paraprofessional can do some legal work independently, in contrast to a Paralegal who must work under the supervision of one or more attorneys.

Parenting Coordinator

Parenting Coordinators help parents work together to parent their children. Parenting Coordinators usually work with high conflict parents after the divorce. However, parenting coordinators can help before and during the divorce as well.

Parenting Time

The time each parent spends with the child or children. Sometimes this is still referred to as "visitation." Visitation is not a great term, because what the parents are doing is parenting, not visiting. For that reason, there has been an effort to move away from using the term "visitation," but your attorney may still use the term visitation.

If one parent has primary physical care, the time the other parent spends with the children will usually be called parenting time or visitation.

Pendente Lite

See Temporary Matters Hearing.

Petition

The Petition is the legal document that, once filed, begins the divorce. The Petition sets out what is being asked of the court. The Petition needs to be served on the Respondent either through acceptance of service or process service.

Petitioner

The Petitioner is the person who filed the Petition, the person who initiated the divorce.

Pretrial Conference

During the divorce process, the court may set a pretrial conference for various reasons. Sometimes the pretrial conference is set to make sure the parties have complied with pretrial requirements. Sometimes a pretrial conference may be set to work out deadlines for things like discovery, witness lists, and other matters.

Pretrial conferences are different from hearings and trial in that they are not evidentiary, meaning that evidence and testimony are not usually a part of a pretrial conference. Pretrial conferences are not typically held to work out issues in the case, but rather to work out logistics.

Other conferences may be set for specific reasons, such as a trial scheduling conference which is held for the express purpose of setting the trial date, length, and sometimes the pretrial deadlines. Courts may also set status conferences or settlement conferences.

If any kind of conference is set in your case, it is likely not evidentiary in nature, and you can ask your attorney what the conference will address if it is not apparent by the name of the conference.

Primary Care

See Custody.

Production of Documents

As part of the discovery process you may be served with Requests for Production of Documents. This will be a list of documents that are relevant to the issues in your divorce that still need to be resolved. The other party will want you to produce the documents or make them available to inspect of copy. Like other parts of discovery (see Interrogatories, Admissions, and Depositions), your attorney will advise you on what requests you will need to respond to and what requests can be objected to.

Pro Se

When a party does not hire an attorney and is representing themselves, they are called "Pro Se" which is Latin for "for yourself."

Process Service

The Petitioner must prove that the Respondent has received the Petition and other documents required by the court. Anyone can give the documents to the Respondent if they are willing to sign an Acceptance of Service that can be filed with the court. If the Respondent will not sign an Acceptance of Service, the Petitioner can have another person give the documents to the Respondent.

The person who gives the documents to the Respondent, often called the process server, will sign an Affidavit of Service that can be filed with the court that states they have given or "served" the documents on the Respondent. Your attorney will likely have someone they typically use as a process server. The process server must be a third party, meaning they cannot be the Petitioner, the Petitioner's attorney, or anyone else who might have an interest in the outcome of the case. Your state may have additional rules on who can be a process server. Usually, your local sheriff can be paid to serve documents, this can be especially useful if you are representing yourself.

Qualified Domestic Relations Order (QDRO)

A QDRO is an order that divides retirement plans that are governed by a federal law called ERISA. The order instructs the plan administrator on the rights of the alternate payee, the spouse that is not a direct participant in the plan. The order can require the plan to divide the participant's account, setting aside an amount or percentage of an amount for the benefit of the alternate payee. The order cannot require the plan to do anything that the plan would not do for the participant. For example, if you have a 401k and have agreed to split the balance of that account with your spouse, you will need a QDRO to order the plan administrator to carry out the terms of your agreement. The plan administrator will need very detailed instructions in the order, and each plan has its own rules on what must be in that order. Sometimes the instructions the plan administrator requires have not been agreed on in the divorce decree, so it is important to go over what the plan might require before the agreement is final. Some things you may need to consider are the value date of the account, who will pay any fees associated with the QDRO, and whether any outstanding loans should be added back into the value of the account. Sometimes a plan administrator will review a proposed QDRO to make sure it has everything the plan administrator will need before being sent to the judge for signature. There may be fees charged by the plan to preapprove a QDRO and to process the final QDRO.

Restraining Order

See No Contact Order

Request for Admissions

See Admissions

Request for Interrogatories

See Interrogatories

Request for Production of Documents

See Production of Documents

Respondent

The Respondent is the party to the case that did not file the Petition. The Respondent is the party that is served with the Petition and other documents. The Respondent will have a set amount of time to respond to the Petition, typically by filing an Answer to the Petition.

Retainer

In an hourly fee arrangement, attorneys typically ask for an advance payment called a retainer. The amount will usually represent the amount of time the attorney thinks they will need to complete the case, multiplied by the attorney's hourly fee. The engagement or retainer agreement should specify under what circumstances you may be required to provide additional funds for your retainer.

The retainer funds will be placed in the attorney or firm's trust account, which is separate from the operating account. Your attorney will pay themselves from the retainer after sending you an invoice to show what was earned during that period of time. If there is money left in your retainer at the end of the case, that amount should be refunded to you. If there is money in your retainer and you decide to stop pursuing the case or you want to hire a different attorney, that money should be refunded to you or sent to the new attorney.

Attorneys who work on an hourly basis require retainers because, if they have made a general appearance on your case and you stop paying their fees, they are not guaranteed to be able to withdraw from your case. The judge may require that they continue to represent you, especially if a trial or important hearing is coming up.

In states where attorneys are allowed to make limited appearances, they may be able to end that appearance without permission of the court. Therefore, they may be able to collect only the amount needed for the agreed-on work instead of a retainer meant to cover the entire case.

Settlement Conference

A formal Settlement Conference may be set by the court, or it may be required that the attorneys for the parties have an informal Settlement Conference to settle a specific issue before the court will schedule a hearing. For instance, sometimes during the discovery process the attorneys may disagree on what must be answered and what can be objected to. The court may require that the attorneys attempt to settle the matter in an informal Settlement Conference before the court will set a hearing date on the issue.

Shared Care

See Custody.

Spousal Support

Also called alimony or spousal maintenance. The court may order spousal support, or the parties may agree that one party will pay the other a monthly amount for support. Some states have a spousal support calculator or formula to calculate spousal support.

There are several types of spousal support that may have different names in different states. Traditional spousal support is usually a set amount of money paid each month for the life of the person paying (payor) or the life of the person receiving (payee). For spousal support to continue through the payee's life, life insurance that will pay the spousal support after the payor's death needs to be put in place.

Rehabilitative spousal support is usually money paid each month for a set period of time, meant to provide support to one spouse while they are reviving their career or going to school to pursue a career.

Stipulation

If an agreement is reached on any or all issues in a divorce, those agreements can be put in a document called a Stipulation (sometimes called Stipulation and Agreement or Agreement). The Stipulation can then be reviewed by the judge. If the judge approves the Stipulation, they can incorporate it into their final ruling or decree, and it becomes a court order. If all issues are resolved by agreement and the judge approves of the resulting Stipulation, then they will enter an Order or Decree dissolving the marriage.

Subpoenas

Subpoenas are orders that require the party receiving them to appear in court or to produce documents. Either party in the divorce can serve subpoenas on organizations or individuals that have information that is important to the case or who will be called as witnesses in a trial. Some witnesses may not need a subpoena because they have agreed to testify or want to testify. However, your attorney may send them a subpoena to make sure they appear on the day of trial. Other witnesses may be willing to testify but require a subpoena to fulfill their own profession's ethical requirements or to satisfy their employer's requirements.

Temporary Matters Hearing

Many courts are overwhelmed with cases that need to be heard. That means that your divorce could take a year or more. Your attorney can file a Motion for a Temporary Matters Hearing to temporarily resolve issues such as custody, child support, spousal support, legal fees, access to or use of property, whether assets can or cannot be sold, and anything else that needs immediate, temporary resolution before the divorce can be finalized. A Temporary Matters Hearing may also be called a Pendente Lite Hearing.

Some courts will allow limited evidence to determine temporary matters. However, the court will likely limit what evidence it will consider or limit the time that you will have to present your evidence, because the court does not want to have a trial before a trial. Some courts will decide temporary matters on affidavit only, meaning that both parties will be allowed to submit an affidavit and possibly supporting material in written form. On the day of the hearing, the court may allow each party's attorney to make a brief statement or argument and then the court will issue an Order that must be followed until the final order is entered in the case.

Trial

If you and the other party cannot come to an agreement, any issues that are still unresolved will go to trial. Trial can be a scary word and conjure all kinds of ideas from television and movies. Trial in a divorce case is not as scary as you might imagine. Unless you are in Texas, there will be no jury and, usually, the only people in the court room will be you, your attorney, your spouse, your spouse's attorney, the judge, a court reporter, a judicial assistant, and people you or your spouse may have brought for support. Witnesses may be there, but they are usually asked to wait in the hall until it is their turn to testify.

Trial Scheduling Conference

A trial scheduling conference is held expressly for the purpose of setting a date (or dates) for trial. If you are represented by an attorney, you may not need to appear for the conference. Based on the dates chosen for the trial, other deadlines may be set. For instance, a deadline for discovery to be concluded, a deadline to file and exchange witness and exhibits list, and a deadline to name any expert that you intend to use. A Trial Scheduling Conference may be held by phone or by other virtual means.

Unbundled Legal Services

Every divorce is different. You may need all the services described in this book or you may only need a few. Unbundled legal services mean that you can pick and choose the parts of your divorce that you want to hire an attorney to handle. Unbundled legal services can be more cost effective.

However, even if you end up paying an attorney for each step of your divorce, with unbundled legal services you have more options. You will also know what each component of your divorce costs.

When you visit an attorney regarding a divorce, they will usually evaluate your case and tell you what the total amount will be to retain them. What goes into that calculation is what services you are likely to need. For instance, is it likely you will need a temporary matters hearing? Will there be extensive discovery? Will there be mediation? The attorney will make a rough calculation of what services you need and how long those services will take, then multiply the estimated hours by their hourly rate to give you a total retainer number. Sometimes attorneys will give you the total number of hours including a trial, even though divorce cases go to trial in only a very small percentage of cases. The retainer may be a very high number and is usually required to be paid in one lump sum before services can begin.

In contrast, if you meet with an attorney that offers unbundled legal services, they will go over the individual services they offer, which ones you are likely to need, and what each one will cost. The cost may be a flat fee, or it may be a retainer for that service, meaning the attorney is still charging you by the hour and the amount collected represents an estimate of the time that service will take. You are then able to choose which services you want the attorney to handle. You may also want to hire the attorney for a few beginning services, see how it goes, and then decide whether to hire the attorney for more services.

Uncontested

A divorce is uncontested if both parties agree on the resolution of all issues. Attorneys charge lower retainers or flat fees for uncontested divorces because discovery, mediation, and trial preparation will not be needed. The hourly rate the attorney will charge will be the same, but the estimate of how much time it will take will be reduced accordingly.

Visitation

See Parenting Time.

About The Author

I HAVE BEEN GUIDING PEOPLE through family law, criminal law, juvenile law, and appellate law systems since graduating from Drake University and receiving my J.D. with honors in May 2009.

I have an undergraduate degree in English and Psychology from the University of Iowa.

I'm on a continuous quest to find the best education, tools, and experience to best help my clients. To that end, I have also become a Certified Mediator, a Certified Collaborative Law Attorney, a Certified Divorce Financial Analyst (CDFA®), and a Certified Life Coach.

I have practiced in private law firms, nonprofit organizations, and for the State of Iowa as an Assistant Attorney General in the Child Support Recovery Unit.

I started my solo practice, Greenberg Law, in 2011. Greenberg Law has grown into Greenberg Law, PLLC.

I provide compassionate, proficient, and forthright legal representation and coaching services. You can feel comfortable telling me about your circumstances knowing that I will not judge you, and I will be straightforward with you about your legal options and likely outcomes.

I am passionate about helping individuals and their families successfully navigate through the family law system.

www.ingramcontent.com/pod-product-compliance
Lightning Source LLC
Chambersburg PA
CBHW050113170426
43198CB00014B/2561